BRITANNIA
The Story of a Mine

By Bruce Ramsey

Original Foreword
Hon. Wesley Black

Introduction by
S. Frank Bruce

First published by
BRITANNIA BEACH COMMUNITY CLUB, 1967
Second Edition by
BC Museum of Mining, 2004
Third Edition by
Britannia Mine Museum, 2014

First Printing

Copyright 1967 by Britannia Beach Community Club, the publishers
Cover design by Kathleen Malloy
Composition and illustrations by Frank Bruce.
Printed in Vancouver, Canada by Agency Press Limited
1020 Hornby Street, Vancouver, BC

Second Printing

© Copyright 2004 The Britannia Beach Historical Society. All rights reserved.

Third Printing

2014 Copyright is by the Britannia Mine Museum Society

Order this book online at www.trafford.com
or email orders@trafford.com

Most Trafford titles are also available at major online book retailers.

© Copyright 1967 by Britannia Beach Community Club,
2004 The Britannia Beach Historical Society,
2014 printing is by the Britannia Mine Museum Society
All rights reserved. No part of this publication may be reproduced, stored in a
retrieval system, or transmitted, in any form or by any means, electronic, mechanical,
photocopying, recording, or otherwise, without the written prior permission of the author.

Printed in the United States of America.

ISBN: 978-1-4120-2836-3 (sc)

Because of the dynamic nature of the Internet, any web addresses or links contained in
this book may have changed since publication and may no longer be valid. The views
expressed in this work are solely those of the author and do not necessarily reflect the
views of the publisher, and the publisher hereby disclaims any responsibility for them.

Any people depicted in stock imagery provided by Thinkstock are models,
and such images are being used for illustrative purposes only.
Certain stock imagery © Thinkstock.

Trafford rev. 05/19/2014

 www.trafford.com
North America & international
toll-free: 1 888 232 4444 (USA & Canada)
fax: 812 355 4082

ABOUT THE AUTHOR:

Bruce Ramsey, author of "Britannia: The Story of a Mine," is a native British Columbian whose own story begins in Nakusp, in the West Kootenays. He is the author of several books on B.C., including "PGE: Railway to the North," "Historic Barkerville," "A History of the German - speaking People of British Columbia" and "Mining in Focus." At the time of the book's first edition, he was on the editorial page staff of the Vancouver Province and is a former chairman of Vancouver Section, British Columbia Historical Association.

ORIGINAL PUBLISHER'S ACKNOWLEDGEMENTS

When this book was first discussed, it was assumed that there must be a mine of available material in the experiences, memories and records of many still living here and elsewhere. At the same time, it was agreed that the success of the project would depend largely on the interest and co-operation of these many contributors. We need not have been concerned about the production end of it - the response was magnificent. Our sincere thanks go to these kind people and to the many individuals and groups who did the hard work of sifting and editing the material.

We single out for special mention the Federal Government Centennial Committee and the B.C. Provincial Government Centennial Committee for their interest, sponsorship and prompt financial support.

To the Anaconda Company (Canada) Limited our thanks are extended for assistance generally and for their co-operation in allowing access to invaluable historical records and materials.

In particular, our grateful thanks go to Archie T. Smith who copied several hundred of his large collection of historical pictures to a uniform size. From these the final selection was made. Smith's contribution ranks next to the manuscript.

The Centennial Committee of the Club, too, merits special mention for the valuable work done since its inception two years ago. We congratulate the Committee on its achievement.

- BRITANNIA BEACH COMMUNITY CLUB

CONTENTS

1. PREHISTORY AND CAPTAIN VANCOUVER
   Geology came first. Volcanic heat and glacial cold. Early man at Boundary Bay. H.M.S. Britannia. Capt. Vancouver's log.
2. THE MINE STARTS FROM SCRATCH
   Britannia's cattle trail. Dr. Forbes finds Britannia copper. Claims and counter-claims. The Company takes form.
3. A DICTATOR IN CAMP
   Britannia M. & S. Company Ltd. Formed. 1908. Regime of John Wedderburn Dunbar Moodie begins. Camp 1050 disaster.
4. FIRE AND FLOOD
   Wartime and postwar years. Copper takes a dive. Loss of the concentrator. Flood disaster strikes the Beach.
5. SPUN YARN AND GROG
   Britannia's navy, "Quadra" and "Princess Louise," Rum running. Seven cases of whisky to Davy Jones.
6. THOROUGH SPINDRIFT TO SAFE PORT
   Stormy Donohue weather, Halycon days of Carleton Perkins Browning commence. Modernization, 1926 style. 1929 Boom and Bust. Pilot C.P. Browning saves the ship. The shadow of Hitler.
7. MINE-MILL ONE OF THE FAMILY
   Pillow-pigeons in the double-deckers. Safety sweepstakes. Wartime comes to Camp, and Harvey Murphy comes to the surface with Mine-Mill Local 663. The War ends.
8. ANACONDA COMES OVER THE RIM-ROCK
   Difficult times. The General Strike, 1946. C.P. Browning leaves. Zinc turns up smiling. The clouds gather. Britannia M. & S. Company wound up. Ghost-town on the mountain. A strike - and a new life with Anaconda.
9. TRAILS AFLOAT AND ASHORE
   Romance of Howe Sound travel. Captain Cates' navy. Japanese railroaders. Roads and trails. PG.E. Railway and Vancouver highway arrive.
10. LOOKING BOTH WAYS
    The Townsite sleeps. Beach life and times. How to win at baseball. Britco News tells all. The Poet of South Valley. Bears in the pantry. Scouts, priests and actors. Valedictory.

VICTORIA

May 5, 1967

Since the presence of copper in the mountains behind Britannia Beach was discovered in 1898 it is estimated that about 60,000 men have been employed there. Some have worked for a grubstake, some have found Britannia a place for summer employment, some have worked off and on as they drifted from mine to mine and some came with their families and stayed until retirement.

Many stories could be told of life in what, for so long, were the isolated camps that comprised Britannia Mines. This book by the well known historian, Bruce Ramsey, attempts, for the first time within our knowledge, to collect and preserve the historical data and some of the anecdotal material. It will be a source of accurate information for the curious and interested and a stimulus to the recollection of happy memories for the legion of ex-Britannia-ites. As one of the latter, having taught school at the old Townsite in the '40's, and as Executive Council member on the Board of Directors of the British Columbia Centennial Committee, I have a personal interest in this book. I trust it will bring you pleasure too.

Provincial Secretary

1966 CENTENARY OF THE UNION OF THE COLONIES OF VANCOUVER ISLAND AND BRITISH COLUMBIA UNDER THE NAME BRITISH COLUMBIA
1967 CENTENARY OF THE CONFEDERATION OF CANADA

FOREWORD TO 2014 REPRINT

It is a privilege and a pleasure to write the foreword to this third reprinting of Britannia, The Story Of A Mine. It is a privilege because I have an opportunity to share a thought on Britannia's history and the role the Britannia Mine Museum has played in preserving this history. It is a pleasure because I have the greatest respect for the individuals who have worked and lived at Britannia; hearing and knowing their stories has enriched my life.

Britannia, The Story of a Mine remains the primary source of information on Britannia's history before 1967, when the book was first published as a project for Canada's Centennial. The Britannia Centennial Committee members were: J. C. Moore, Mary Smith, Olive Baxter, Hugh Chisholm, Dave Clark, Joan Ehler, Alice Graney, Betty McNair, and W.B. Montgomery. The BC Museum of Mining, as it was called in 2004, reprinted the book in celebration of 100 years of Britannia Beach history. Today, after another 10 years passing, the Museum is again reprinting this book with a new epilogue, an updated index which lists in one place all the Britannia people in the book and a new cover. Each printing represents a moment of reflection about Britannia Beach and Mount Sheer.

In 1967 the community was characterized as a company town, under Anaconda's management. Mount Sheer as a place to live had been 'closed' a few years previously because mining operations were consolidating. As characterized by the Centennial Committee, residents cared deeply about the place they called home. No one could have anticipated what the next 47 years brought. In 2004 the community was emerging from years as an 'orphan', which is perhaps an appropriate description for the period between 1974 and 2004 when the Village was no longer a company town in the true sense. Britannia had few resources; residents fought hard for everything they needed and there was a tarnish associated with the negative environmental legacy from mining. In 2004 the future was indeed brighter and much had changed for residents and businesses. Environmental remediation and fee simple land ownership was imminent. Today, in 2014 and a mere 10 years later, the community has many amenities and the Museum too has benefited from major investment from both government and the mining industry.

This printing includes two epilogues. The new one (2014), which is co-authored by Jane Iverson and Diane Mitchell summarizes well the achievements and trials of Britannia. Each period in Britannia's history is deserving of its own book, yet to be written, because there are so many perspectives to be told.

There are many reasons why I am proud of the Britannia Mine Museum. Despite our own challenges we have preserved important stories of this community. The stories of the people who worked and lived here are peppered throughout our exhibits and tours and give our visitors a true sense of place and identity. The Museum's photo collection contains more than 9000 images of social and mining history and with the archive of papers and memorabilia we have a rich resource we can rely on. The skills and qualifications of the staff of the Museum have matured so we can rightly claim being credible experts in many areas including the history of Britannia Beach/Mount Sheer but also environmental education and mining in general. Those who work at the Museum are motivated to find the impactful ways to give our visitors a sense of history of a richly storied place and the modern context of mining and its importance to our everyday living. The republishing of this book is just one of our many programs that do this.

In our modern world change is a constant. For those of us who work at the Museum we have been blessed with a constant theme. Rarely a day goes by when there isn't an email, phone call, letter, or visitor who takes the time to tell us their personal connection to the place we work. In closing, I give a heartfelt thank you to these many people who I call my Britannia friends.

Kirstin Clausen
Executive Director, Britannia Mine Museum

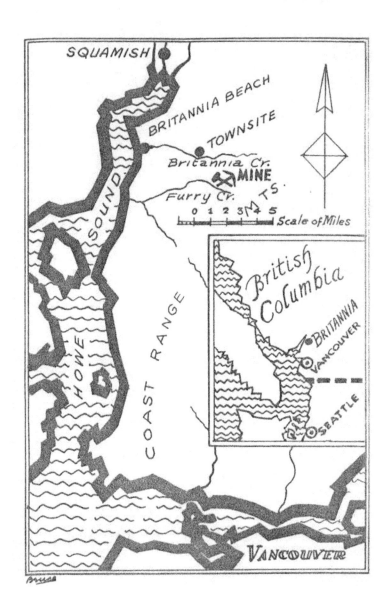

INTRODUCTION

This is a story of the far Canadian West. As far west as one can go along the Canadian - United States mainland border, and a few miles north, lies Vancouver, British Columbia's largest city and principal Pacific port.

On a touring map the little village of Britannia appears to be almost in the suburbs of Vancouver. Actually, is it a good thirty-five miles along Howe Sound, north from the big city - just a nice drive. For most of the period covered by this book there was no connecting road, nor railway, only the Union Steamships. The journey took most of the day.

The coast is not unlike that of Norway, heavily indented, trenched by the ice long gone, thickly forested, the peaks snowy for most of the year, swirling with mist, continually washed up by the cold from the North. The thirty miles of Howe Sound water, chilled by the glacial streams, can be placid or frighteningly rough. Except for the scars of road and railway and logged-off areas, there is a little sign of human occupation or effort. The precipitous islands and mainland mountains stand dreaming as they have through the ages, with feet in the cold waves, shoulders to the wind. Across the water from Britannia, the pulp mill town of Woodfibre is only a cloud of smoke by day, a glimmer at night. Squamish, loggers, beer parlors and bright stores, lies seven miles north around the bend.

A gravelly estuary of the Britannia Creek provided the site for the Beach Community, one of the few open spaces on many miles of coastline. With about two hundred families, Britannia is today still a "company" town in appearance. There's no shopping street, no bus depot, no town hall, no police station. Fires are put out by the volunteer brigade. The general store, post office, school, church and gas station keep things going. Company resources grade, paint up, fence, clean up, replace, improve. High on the hill are the houses of the staff, quite modern, with a long view of the Sound and the lofty, romantic islands twenty miles south. Down by the sea the houses are frame built, neatly painted and fenced, some quite old. Near the school and church is a street of new homes, four to a unit. On one quiet street are several new white trailer homes, tree-shaded and fenced with white pickets. Children are everywhere, and their clothes swing like flags on every line. Only the luckiest dogs live at Britannia and they too are all around. Trees venture down the steep hillsides and embrace the houses. Shade trees share with office buildings, church and club. Below its wooden bridges brawls Britannia Creek, rusty red and longing to get away from it all.

The people are like people everywhere in outlying places. They dress to suit conditions, warm even rough things in winter, caps and mackinaws. In season, informal colorful togs, neat enough for visiting, ready for a ball game or fishing or polishing something. Most drive good cars, the fathers washing and polishing when the sun shines, the children helping. Voices around store and post-office are hearty; many have been friends for years. On warm days, the benches on the store porch attract off-duty workers or old-timers. Dogs wait. Mothers clutch grocery bags and call kids. Teenagers chatter, arms full of books. Nothing is new or very different, but it is all Britannia. It is all very much as it has been since the early days, a place to live and work, to raise kids, to eat and drink with friends, to share one's life with others, to talk shop.

Mainly it is the road that makes the difference. Once an isolated coast community, Britannia has become a wide spot on the highway and part of a much larger mobile community. At weekends adventurous hordes throng by, Britannia merely a milestone. On weekdays the road is busy with workers, salesmen, trucks, trailers. Far out on the water ply fishboats, tugs with scows, rafts of logs, the gulls and black crows circling, passing. Encompassing it all are the watchful mountains, sunny and beckoning one day, story, clouded and aloof a day later, never the same.

After well over sixty years Britannia is still a producing mine and a thriving community. When I first worked here in the mid-thirties, she had produced by then half a billion tons of copper, owned 25,000 acres of claims, had spent ten million dollars for property, plant and buildings. Through the years she has produced steadily and maintained her place as one of British Columbia's great copper mines. Recent location of new ore reserves in the Mine seems to indicate a prosperous future.

Britannia's story is the old story of hard work overcoming obstacles. Management and the labor force, the Government, the owners, the claim-jumpers and their friends and Nature herself, all put in their car. The story of it all is Bruce Ramsey's in the pages of his history.

S.Frank Bruce,

Britannia, B.C. 1967

1

PREHISTORY AND CAPTAIN VANCOUVER

THE YEARS OF human experience we will touch upon in this book are but a fleeting moment, possibly exciting to us, but merely a moment of no importance in the great span of Time. We talk about events of the past 100 years as being "a long time ago", but look to the hills and to the rocks and ask, "what is 100 years in comparison to 175 million years? Further, what is 175 million years to the phase of our history which opens with the words, "In the beginning...?"

In the infinitesimal flicker of time since 1867 we have called some periods "cataclysmic", but again we must ask a question. What are these man-made catastrophes, such as wars and nuclear bombs, in comparison to the cataclysms which moulded the mountains, the inlets of the sea and the very land we stand upon?

There are no printed pages to tell us the story of what happened 175 million years ago. But nature has left us a record, scarred and seared into the rocks, which the geologist can read. These ancient marks of cataclysm around Britannia are the reasons for Britannia Beach's existence today.

The earth was already old by our standards, and even by the standards of Time, 175 million years ago. Great wind-swept waves rolled across the shallow seas which covered this part of the world while, deep down in the bowels of the earth, forces beyond human comprehension were stirring, and, in the process of time, they broke loose as volcanoes and spewed lava and ashes into the pre-historic sea to give foundation to a new land.

Then followed a period of relative peace, but not a period of inactivity. Wind and rain beat down on the land, and like a sculptor, carved, or rather eroded away the original stark outline. In these few words we have covered millions of years and there would still be millions yet to come before man would make his appearance.

Again there was a cataclysmic period, this one appeared about 75 million years ago. Granitic intrusions engulfed and partially digested the earlier volcanics and the sediments created by erosion. In great upheavals the rocks were folded, faulted and altered. Dikes and sills of granite material cut through the rocks of 175 million years ago as if they were but paper, and while all this was going on, another strange and wonderful process of nature was in action. Solutions carrying copper, zinc, iron, sulphur and gold were introduced into the older, folded and downwarped sedimentary rocks. The Britannia copper-zinc ore deposits were formed.

And as though nature tired of cataclysms and needed a rest from her labors, once more we find the process of creation left to erosion; and millions of years rolled by.

Then, in what seems like recent history by comparison, a mere 500,000 years ago, this whole area was engulfed under a vast sheet of ice which covered the land to a staggering elevation of about 5000 feet. As the ice formed into glaciers, it moved and cut into the earth's surface, scouring, carving and marking forever the age-old rocks. During this ice-age, which lasted approximately 475,000 years, volcanoes once more erupted and poured out lava, and even after the ice had retreated, these mountains of fire and brimstone continued to change the face of the land. The last eruption in this area took place 10,000 years ago, although Mount Baker to the south has erupted in historical times.

One final step took place before nature saw that her creation was good. Since the retreat of the ice 25,000 years ago, the land surface has risen to a maximum of 500 to 800 feet. Erosion again took over and once more took up its relentless carving, as it continues to do to this day.

Now the time has arrived for man to make his appearance. We do not know when the first human gazed at the mountains which are now so familiar to us, nor do we know who he was, where he came from, where he went, nor what he looked like. But 2000 years ago one of these ancients was buried at Boundary Bay and on his chest was placed a copper breastplate, which may or may not have come from Britannia. It does show, however, that copper was important even in those ancient days.

The people who followed this Very Important Person at Boundary Bay, and probably those who came before him, were warrior people, accustomed to being on the receiving end or the giving end of murderous raids. And strangely enough, this primitive way of life was carried on in another part of the world they never imagined to even exist. Here warfare was carried on on a far larger scale, but in both cases, it was sea-power which counted.

Towards the end of what the Europeans called the 18th Century two mighty forces faced each other. They too, had their ships, big ones, tall in the sail, which rode the seas like great floating castles, and there were the little ones, larger than those of the Indians to be sure, which bobbed up and down like corks in the same sea the monarchs rode with such dignity.

On the one side there was His Most Christian Majesty Charles III of Spain, whose naval pride was the *San Josef*, 112 guns, 2,457 tons, which even the British Navy was reluctantly forced to admit was the finest ship afloat. One naval historian has said of the *San Josef* that she united "all the superior qualities of a ship of the line with the sailing of the fastest frigate; her lower deck ports were higher with all her seastores in than was ever known in any other ship of the line; and she could carry her guns run-out when few British ships would have ventured to open a port; she stowed 600 tons of water, and we had nothing that could compare to her as a ship of war."

On the other side was the fleet of His Britannic Majesty George IV, an impressive fleet to be sure, and amongst this array of sea power was H.M.S. *Britannia*, 100 guns, and certainly not to be compared with the *San Josef*. *Britannia* was launched in 1762 and had taken part in skirmishes connected with the American War of Independence where she had lumbered along, picking up as she went the nickname "Old Ironsides" a name which was not as complimentary as that given to the American's U.S.S. *Constitution*.

Besides the ships, there were of course, the sea dogs of great repute; men of such caliber as John Jervis, Don Francisco Xavier, Winthuysen, Horatio Nelson, Richard Scrope Howe, Earl Howe, and Alexander Hood, names which even today are toasted in grog wherever old naval battles are refought.

While the powderkeg of Europe was awaiting the signal to explode, tiny vessels of Britain and Spain, scarcely larger than a modern tug boat, were at work mapping the new found territories of the west coast of what is now British Columbia. As they surveyed this jagged coastline of fjords, islands and channels, they gave to us of the 20th Century a legacy of shining names in naval history by placing them on their charts. Thus to the expedition of Don Jose Eliza we owe the name San Josef Bay on the northern tip of Vancouver Island, and the men of this voyage of exploration were also the first of the white race to enter the harbor of what we know today as Nanaimo and Departure Bay. To this inlet they gave the name Winthuysen, by which it was known as late as 1853.

In June 1792, Captain George Vancouver, RN, appeared in these waters, and after leaving his sloop-of-war *Discovery* at Birch Bay proceeded north by longboat where after naming Point Atkinson "after a particular friend" he proceeded up Howe Sound, and as he states in his Journal "we passed on the western shore some detached rocks, with some sunken ones against them, that extend about two miles, but are not so far from the shore as to impede navigation of the sound, up which we made a rapid progress, by the assistance of a fresh southerly gale, attended with dark gloomy weather, that greatly added to the dreary prospect of the surrounding country. The low fertile shores we had been accustomed to see, though lately with some interruption, here no longer existed; their place was now occupied by the base of the stupendous snowy barrier, thinly wooded, and rising from the sea abruptly to the clouds, from whose frigid sides, the dissolving snow in foaming torrents rushed down the sides and chasms of its rugged surface, exhibiting altogether a sublime though gloomy spectacle, which animated nature seemed to have deserted. Not a bird, nor a living creature was to be seen, and the roaring of the falling cataracts in every direction precluded their being heard, had any been in the neighborhood.

"Towards noon," Captain Vancouver continues, "I considered that we had advanced some miles within the western boundary of the snowy barrier as some of its rugged, lofty mountains were now behind, and to the southward of us. This filled my mind with the pleasing hope of finding our way to its eastern side. The sun shining at this time for a few minutes afforded an opportunity of ascertaining the latitude of the east point of the island which, from the shape of the mountain which composes it, obtained the name 'Anvil Island' to be 40°30', its longitude 237°3'. We passed an island the forenoon of Friday the 15th, lying on the eastern shore, opposite to an opening on the western, which evidently led into the gulf nearly in a S.W. direction, through a numerous assemblage of rocky islands and rocks, and also another opening to the westward of this island, that seemed to take a similar direction. Between Anvil Island and the north point of the first opening, which lies from hence S by W five miles distance, are three rocky islets, lying about a mile from the western shore. The width of this branch of the sound is about a league, but northward form Anvil Island it soon narrows to half that breadth, taking a direction N.N.E. as far as latitude 49°39', longitude 237°9', where all our expectations vanished, in finding it to terminate in a round basin, encompassed on every side by the dreary country already described. At its head and on the upper part of the eastern shore a narrow margin of low land runs from the foot of the mountain barrier to the waterside, which produces a few dwarf pine trees, with some little variety of underwood. The water of the sound was here nearly fresh, and in colour a few shades darker than milk; this I attributed to the melting of the snow, and its water passing rapidly over a chalky surface, which appeared probably by the white aspect of some of the chasms that seemed formerly to have been the course of waterfalls but are now dry.

"The gap," Captain Vancouver continues, "we had entered in the snowy barrier seemed of little importance, as through the valleys, caused by the irregularity of the mountain's tops, other mountains more distant, and apparently more elevated, were seen rearing their heads in various directions. In this dreary and comfortless region, it was no inconsiderate piece of good fortune to find a little cove in which we could erect our tent; as we had scarcely finished our examination when heavy squalls and torrents of rain, which continuing until noon the following day, Friday the 15th, occasioned a very unpleasant detention. But for the circumstances we might too hastily have concluded that this part of the gulf was uninhabited. In the morning we were visited by nearly forty natives, on whose approach, from the very material alteration that had now taken place in the face of the country, we expected to find some difference in their general character. This conjecture was however, premature, as they varied in no respect whatever, but in possession of a more ardent desire for commercial transactions; into the spirit of which they entered with infinitely more avidity than any of our former acquaintances, not only in bartering amongst themselves the different valuables they had obtained from us, but when the trade became slack, in exchanging those article again with our people; in which traffic they always took care to gain some advantage and would frequently exult on the occasion. Some fish, their garments, spears, bows and arrows to which these people wisely added their copper ornaments, comprised their general stock in trade. Iron in all its forms, they judiciously preferred to any other article we had to offer.

"The weather permitting us to proceed, we directed our route along the continental or western shore of the sound, passing within two small islands and the main island, into the opening before mentioned, stretching to the westward from Anvil Island. At the distance of one hundred yards from the shore, the bottom could not be reached within 60 fathoms of line, nor had we been able to gain soundings in many places since we had quitted Point Atkinson with 80 and 100 fathoms though it was frequently attempted; except at the basin at the head of the sound, where the depth suddenly decreased from 60 fathoms to two. We had advanced a short distance only in this branch, before the color of the water changed from being nearly milky white and almost fresh, to that of oceanic and perfectly salty. By sunset we had passed the channel which had been observed to lead into the gulf, to the southward of Anvil Island; and about nine o'clock landed for the night, near the west point of entrance into the sound, which I distinguished by the name of Howe Sound, in honor of Admiral Earl Howe."

Vancouver now turned north and on June 19 reached "an arm of sea" which "I gave the name Jervis's channel" in honour of Admiral Sir John Jervis…"

Thus are enshrined, in the years 1791 and 1792, the names of brave men and their ships, and who was to know that within the decadal year they would be pitted against each other in combat which was to be the beginning of the end for the loser as a maritime power.

And *Britannia*, the second ship to bear the proud name, was to win her battle honors.

Meanwhile, *Britannia*, lumbering along as usual, had been on patrol in the Mediterranean from 1793 to 1794 flying the flag of Admiral William Hotham, second in command to Lord Hood. Here the situation was particularly dangerous to British interests. The French and Spanish were combining to rule the waves and were even planning to attack England herself. Not since the days of Drake had the situation been so serious. Jervis' job was to see that the attack did not materialize. At dawn, February 14, 1797, off the fog-shrouded Portuguese headland of Cape St. Vincent, Jervis waited.

The fleet under his command numbered fifteen sail-of-the-line of which Victory and *Britannia* mounted 100 guns, the *Barfleur* and *Prince George*, 98 each; *Blenheim* and *Namur*, 90 guns. These were the deckers, the monarchs of the sea. Besides he had the following 74 guns HMS *Culloden*, *Colossus*, *Captain*, *Excellent*, *Egmont*, *Goliath*, *Irrisistable*, and *Orion*. The *Diadem*, of 64 guns, four frigates, a sloop and a cutter completed the array with which Jervis proposed to engage the Spanish Grand Fleet of 27 of-the-line, ten frigates and a brig. Half a dozen of the Spanish three deckers carried 112 guns and the four-decker *Santissima Trinidad*, flagship of Done Jose de Cordoba, mounted 136. Included in the fleet was the *San Josef* and *San Nicolas*, with 80 guns.

Cordoba had not expected to meet up with the British fleet and his line of ships was long and straggling. Before they had time to recover from the shock of seeing the British squadron drawn up in battle formation it was too late. Jervis "flew to them as a hawk to his prey" with the *Culloden* leading the way. Almost immediately the fighting power of the Spanish fleet was broken. In the battle which raged furiously, Horatio Nelson, from *Victory*, headed a boarding party to seize the pride of Charles III, the formidable *San Josef*. When the ship was firmly in British hands, Nelson found Admiral Winthuysen dying below decks.

This action, off Cape St. Vincent, was to be the first of many brilliant victories to be won by Britain's favourite sea-dog, and "San Josef" was later enscribed in Nelson's Coat-of-Arms. *Britannia*, too, showed herself off to a good account, and on reaching home, honors galore were heaped upon the victors who, in a very real sense, had saved England. And in 1859 the auxiliary steam sloop *Plumper*,

Captain George Henry Richards, while surveying Howe Sound, gave the name Britannia to the range of mountains on the eastern shore, a remembrance of a battle fought 62 years before.

Other names of heroes and their ships in the Battle of Cape St. Vincent were also remembered: Hallowell Mountain, Jervis Inlet, honors the Canadian, Benjamin Hallowell, who served in *Victory*; Culloden Point, Troubridge Mountain, after Thomas Troubridge, captain of the *Culloden*; Captain Island, Egmont Point, Goliath Bay, Diadem Mountain, Nelson Island, St. Vincent Bay, Saumarez Bluff, after Captain Sir James Saumarez of HMS *Orion*; Foley Mountain, after Thomas Foley, captain of *Britannia* at the Battle of the St. Vincent. Barfleur Passage in Howe Sound recalls HMS *Barfleur*.

In 1864 another survey ship, the old Hudson's Bay Company Steamer *Beaver*, first steam vessel to ply the north Pacific, was surveying Frederick Arm under command of Captain Daniel Pender, and a 4,200 foot mountain was named in honor of Admiral Winthuysen.

Meanwhile, *Britannia*, the veteran ship of the Royal Navy had one more glorious action in her battle record before she faded away. On October 21, 1805 she was again at Nelson's side and responded to the famous signal "England expects that every man this day will do his duty." This time Britannia was flying the flag of rear Admiral the Earl of Northesk and was commanded by Captain Charles Bullen. Because of her bulk *Britannia*, always a slow starter, had no close encounter with the enemy, and it was only through determined handling on the part of Northesk that she was even able to take part in the battle. Just the same *Britannia's* losses at the Battle of Trafalgar were ten killed and 40 wounded. Her name was then changed to HMS *St. George*, but her name lingers on in one of the most famous copper mines in the world, Britannia.

Britannia Landing, the earliest known photo of Britannia Beach. BMM #13156

Early view of Britannia Camp. BMM #12870

No. 1 Mill, about 1910. BMM #13477

Crushing Section, No. 1 Mill, about 1910. The ore is being delivered by aerial tram. BMM #13479

2
THE MINE STARTS FROM SCRATCH

After the visit of Captain Vancouver 70 years pass by without a recorded visit by a European to the waters of Howe Sound. All this was to change early in 1858 when gold was discovered in the gravels of the Fraser River, just before Fort Yale, a hundred miles upstream from the mouth of the river. As a result of this momentous discovery a town grew up at Point Roberts, just below the Fraser's estuary, called Roberts City, and aside from its saloons, it doesn't appear to have had much going for it.

Perhaps it was because of a villainous concoction served to the miners which would be a libel on the name whisky to call it that, but whatever the reasons, the residents of Roberts City were convinced that the rush to the Fraser was a waste of time and energy. The real gold, they said lay up the Squamish River. The Victoria Gazette tells us of an expedition which set out for the Squamish in search of gold, but the results fell far below expectations and it is not surprising that nothing more is said of the Squamish bonanza. And a year later, Roberts City was as dead as a dodo.

In the early stages of the gold rush a certain John McKay headed a survey party from the head of Lillooet Lake in the Pemberton area, down to Howe Sound and recommended it as a wagon road route to the interior, but Governor James Douglas thought otherwise.

The following year, 1859, as we have seen, HMS *Plumper* was in the vicinity and we can be certain that in the next decade prospectors ranged the Howe Sound country in search of materials.

Evidence of this is contained in a small booklet published in Victoria in 1868 by Leigh Harnett in which he mentions "the Howe Sound Copper Mine near Burrard Inlet." We know very little about Legh Harnett. He came up from California where, he claimed, he had been interested in mining for 17 years. His purpose in coming to British Columbia was "for the purpose of compiling a brief history of the colony" and in 1867, the year of Confederation of the Canadas, he visited the Cariboo. Here is his report on "the Howe Sound Copper Mine."

"His excellency the Governor (Frederick Seymour) was kind enough to place his little steam yacht *Leviathen* at my disposal in order to visit the Howe Sound copper mine, near Burrard Inlet, soon after his discovery. Many in this city (Victoria) have asked me since my return, whether there is anything in it. Indeed there is, you may be assured, a great deal in it. I pronounce it by far the best thing of the kind discovered in the colony and quite as legitimate as any on the Pacific Coast. It is one of four mines hitherto found in the world, of which we have record, where sulphuret ore in a concentrated form was carried in quantity and of high percentage on the surface. Nor is there any doubt in my mind about it being a true organic vein, for there, plainly in sight, are all the essentials necessary to constitute a true copper vein down even to the flucken, the first and last essential. At present there is slight displacement, which will require probably drifting for a hundred feet to overcome. As soon as the vertical dip is reached in the hill the vein will show itself in its true course and form, and at least be three feet thick. If this mine is now judiciously managed by the owners, and liberally dealt with by the government, it must be of immense good to the colony; for it at once establishes the reliability of your vast copper ledges, and may in the end, when thoroughly developed, excel the marvelous riches of the Union in Copperopolis and the Cobra in Cuba, for neither of these celebrated mines were equal to the Howe Sound mine on the surface."

Mr. Harnett gave us plenty of information about this property but neglected, along with the newspaper of the day, to give one essential bit: Where was the mine?

A decade later, the Indian River country, behind Britannia, entered the political – and historical – picture of British Columbia with a bang. In 1873 work was begun on constructing a cattle trail from Lillooet down to Burrard Inlet, reaching the sea at what is now Lillooet Avenue in North Vancouver. For three years the work went steadily on, and the costs went steadily up. In the fall 1877 Robert Carson, the cattle king of Pavillion Mountain, ventured down the trail with a herd of beeves for the market at Hastings Mill, around which the city of Vancouver had beginnings. They succeeded in getting through to Moodyville, now part of North Vancouver, but only after terrible hardships, particularly on the rough, steep and feedless portion of the trail above Cheakamus and through the Indian River country. Carson's cattle were the first and only beeves to come all the way down, for a legislative committee which investigated the project – after $32,250 had been spent on it (and that, in 1877, was an enormous sum of money), found the trail unusable.

At the same time this trail was under construction, Marcus Smith, a civil engineer was examining the Squamish area as a possible route for the Canadian Pacific Railway.

All these events were but preludes to three others, the visit of a dog fisherman by the name of Granger, the subsequent visit of Dr. A. A. Forbes and the death of a buck at sunset. The central figure is Dr. Forbes. Like a later medical man, Dr. W.B. Burnett, of the Cariboo Gold Quartz mine at Wells, Dr. Forbes was at heart anyway, more of a mining man than a physician. Scottish-born, he entered the Royal Navy at the age of 13 and left the service ten years later after cultivating a taste for chemistry. Settling in Connecticut he soon became a school teacher, got married, and then took a medical course, coming to British Columbia in 1886. He died in 1935 at the age of 85.

In 1888 Dr. Forbes was medical officer to the Indians of this region, a practice which took him from Lund to Squamish, and while at Hopkins Landing on Howe Sound, Granger, the dog fisherman, came to see him to put the touch for $400. Years later, on May 17, 1931, Dr. Forbes told Cecil Scott, a reporter with *The Vancouver Province* what took place at that meeting.

"Granger showed me some barren rock on which there was chlorides of copper or nitrate. I told him that was not very encouraging, but there might be some better showing of copper in the vicinity of his find. He was very anxious to buy a boat with his $400 and go to Alaska."

"I'll show you the place for $400." he proposed.

"Well, I told him that if I didn't see better mineral than he had shown me I could not give him anything, but if we found mineral in place I would give him $400. In a few days we made the trip, landing on the other side of the ridge north of the present landing. He was no woodsman and we had a terrible time over that ridge. He took me almost to the summit of the mountain and showed me the spot he had broken the rock from."

"There were few places not covered with snow, but we slept that night on the summit. Next morning I began prospecting around the summit, gradually descending towards the valley, without success. About an hour and a half before sunset I saw the famous buck. I shot him in the neck and he kicked around considerably and when I finally got him killed I found he had kicked the moss and rubbage off the rock and there was some good showing on the surface. It was getting too dark that night to do anything more, but in the morning I put a shot of dynamite I had with me and found I had got a good showing in place. I then and there paid him the $400 on the condition that he would not speak to anyone in Howe Sound or Vancouver about it. He agreed and in a few days he bought his boat and went to Alaska."

"So," Dr. Forbes continued, "the first discoverer of copper on Britannia was Mr. Granger, the second was Mr. Buck and the third was Dr. Forbes."

"When I found the mineral on Britannia Mountain and for many years afterwards, there was little danger in leaving the claim open as no one was looking for any other mineral but gold. As a matter of fact, I was perfectly right in leaving it open, as no one did disturb it for ten years. I visited the property every summer for eight years, working on it for a week, and never saw a human being on or near the mountain except when Mr. Granger was with me."

Dr. Forbes had previously re-discovered an abandoned claim on Mount Elphinstone near Hopkins Landing, and on mentioning it at the Business Men's Club, the forerunner to the Vancouver Club, he learned its tiny tunnel had been put in by one of the early merchants of British Columbia, the Oppenheimers. It is possible that this was the claim Legh Harnett referred to in his report. Later, Dr. Forbes received some samples of ore from Texada Island, and so, in 1893 he went to see the minister of mines in Victoria seeking government aid to assist him in developing one of these claims, either the Elphinstone, Britannia or Texada properties.

"Mr. Pooley," Dr. Forbes continued in his interview with Cecil Scott, "sent out for certain books when I got through and started reading from them. They were reports of geologists about the mineral resources of the country. And their findings were that there were no commercial mineral in the district." With that meeting Dr. Forbes' interest in the Britannia property came to practically an end. He did, however, develop the Texada claims, and subsequently returned to the practice of medicine, becoming medical officer for the Powell River Company, producers of pulp and paper at their townsite of Powell River.

In nearly all stories about mine development there is the sad tale of the poor but honest prospector who is taken to the cleaners by the smart city slickers. Such was the fate of an illiterate trapper by the name of Oliver Furry who had a cabin on McNab Creek on the west side of Howe Sound.

Furry may have heard of Dr. Forbes' find, or he may have seen the doctor coming in or out of the property, but one day while in Vancouver Furry dropped in to see W.A. Clark in his store at Hastings and Carrall. Like Dr. Forbes, Clark was extremely interested in mining, and on this particular day, his counter was cluttered with mining samples. He told Furry that he would be a smart man if, while wandering around the hills in search of game and tending to his trap line, he kept an eye out for mineral showings. Furry was not particularly interested at first, but Clark's persuasion made him change his mind, and he told Clark he knew where there were some showings. As a result of this information Clark proposed paying for Furry's prospecting license, furnish the grubstake and pay the recording fees as well as doing half the assessment work required by law. Then, Clark said, they would share and share alike in any of the claims Furry staked. And so, armed with licenses made out to W.A. Clark, his wife, Bertha, his brother J. F. Clark, Oliver Furry and his brother, Ira, five claims were located, including the famous Jane.

Oliver Furry then trudged back to Vancouver with some 200 pounds of samples and told Clark there was a mountain of ore where he found them. Clark submitted the samples to Barclay Bonthorne who represented a group of Scottish capitalists and who happened to be interested in the mining game. Bonthorne declared they were the finest samples he had seen in the country and he proposed taking an option on the property for $10,000 for further investigation, but regretted he would have to postpone making the deal as he was leaving for Scotland the following day. Bonthorne's judgement was confirmed by J. Sullivan, a Vancouver assayer, who said the samples showed 75 per cent copper.

Meanwhile, in the far northern reaches of the province, a mad stampede was taking place in the Atlin country, and Clark headed north to see what it was all about. While in Atlin he was taken north ill with pneumonia and was confined to bed for several months, so long, in fact, that his assessment work on Britannia Mountain was not done. On his return to Vancouver he found that Furry had taken in Thomas T. Turner, a Vancouver fur buyer, and Joseph Boscowitz, a prominent Victoria fur dealer and businessman, as well as Boscowitz' sons, David and Leopold. In August 1898 Furry had added to his original stakings the Empress, Victoria and Queen mineral claims constituting the Empress group, on the understanding that he was to receive a non-assessable half-interest to the claims. Subsequently Furry received from the Boscowitz family a document to this effect, but signed, with a rubber stamp, "Boscowitz & Sons."

Clark looked up Oliver Furry and it was arranged they return to Britannia and locate other claims. These new stakings were south of the Empress group, one being located in the name of Mrs. Clark, and another in the name of J. Donald of Vancouver, Mrs. Clark's claim was the Charmer, a property she held until disposing of it to the Britannia Mining and Smelting Company for a good price.

An option was taken on these properties by J.C. Keith, one of the Vancouver's first millionaires who, subsequently, was president of the Howe Sound, Pemberton Valley and Northern Railway, the predecessor to the Pacific Great Eastern Railway. Keith ran a tunnel 100 feet in length, but the option was not taken up.

With the staking came the rush. For years ship-owners had gone broke in the Howe Sound area. As early as 1891 John McDonald, a former Vancouver alderman, put the little steamer *Saturna* on the run to haul supplies and mail to Mashiter's store and post office in Squamish. The *Saturna*, formerly owned by the celebrated author and explorer, Warburton Pike, a resident of Saturna Island, was subsequently wrecked. Her successor was the *Burt*, Captain Dan Mooney, but he soon found the run didn't pay and so gave up in disgust leaving the field to Captain J.A. Cates of the Terminal Steam Navigation Company, who placed in service, largely to supply Bowen Island, the steamer *Defiance*. For two years Cates' fortunes hung in the balance, profits were few and far between, but in 1900, with the development of the mines on Britannia, he was able to cash in.

Now that the stampede was underway the sounds of prospectors driving in stakes echoed down Mineral Creek, Thistle Creek, Britannia Creek and Furry Creek. At the site of the present gravel pit, just south of Britannia Beach townsite, a floating pier jutted out into the water to receive passengers from the *Defiance*. From this point a trail headed in a northeasterly direction to the Jane Creek Camp, which then consisted of a couple of log cabins. As the 1050 Camp, this little settlement was to sear itself into the minds of the people of British Columbia fifteen years later. Another trail, the Daisy, turned south at the float and then northeast towards the claims owned by the Goldsmith Copper Company, the Daisy, Hunters Friend, Eureka, Copper Dyke, Copper Canyon, Alice and Annie.

One of the problems faced by Boscowitz was that the landing was on the Copper Dyke property, and of even greater importance, of course, was financing. They decided, therefore, to get rid of the claims and so approached James Findlay, who had operated the Pugsley Mine on Princess Royal Island and he was asked to help find a buyer. One of those contacted was Joseph Adams, a mining engineer from Rossland, B.C. He examined the property and was so favorably impressed by what he saw that he wired Howard S. Walters, of Libby, Montana, that he had found "the biggest mine" he had ever seen.

It was a fortunate time to contact Walters for he had just sold his interests in the Snowshoe Mine at Libby for a good price and at the moment had considerable money to invest. He immediately headed for Vancouver, and with Boscowitz and Findlay took the *Defiance* up to the Landing and looked the ground over for himself. As a result Walters purchased a seven-tenths interest in the property for $35,000.

To operate the property, and to acquire the Walters interests, a meeting was held in rooms at 622 Hastings to approve a memorandum of association for the Britannia Copper Syndicate. The original syndicate consisted of J.T. Hills, Charles McMeekin, CE,

F.M. Leonard, J.W. Lee, L. Adams, John F. Humphreys, Thomas Dunn, H. T. Ceppreley, C.D. Rand and George Bower. The remaining three-tenths interest in the mines was held by the Boscowitz interests.

Of the capital stock of the Britannia Copper Syndicate Ltd., 200 shares were allotted to the members at $125 per share (they met a subsequent call for a further $125) and the rest of the stock was put in the treasury and offered to the public from $800 to $1000 a share.

Within 60 days after organization 100 shares had been sold and development work, under the direction of Howard Walters, was commenced. A drift was made west from the Boscowitz tunnel and ore was struck at 26 feet. This showed an assay of seven percent copper. While doing this work, Walters discovered an outcrop of the Fairview mineral zone to the east of Mammoth Bluff and concluded they had a body of ore probably 250 feet wide and 650 feet in length. It was projected that the outcrop showed an average of two percent copper, with gold running up to $12 a ton. A mistake was made as far as the gold was concerned, but the Fairview property became one of the mainstays of the Britannia mine.

On June 1, 1900, the directors heard a progress report from Walters on work at the mine that "pursuant with their individual advice and approval, he had accomplished the purchase of seventy-five acres of land covering the most desirable water frontage at Britannia Beach, for harbor, plant site and townsite privileges, known at the Leatherdale tract, for the sum of $3,300 net, which sums has been paid."

He also reported that "in view of the uncertainty attaching to the volume of local water supply available…he had deemed it necessary to secure and control Fairy Falls," owned by "Shannon and McLachlan" for $3,500. He said it was capable of generating "500 electric horse power for six months or more per annum."

Walter was also chairman of a committee known as "Committee on Future Policy of the Company" and on June 1, this group informed the stockholders that "they recommend to the stockholders that they authorize their directors to negotiate and conclude a sale of the Britannia Group at a rate of not less than $1,500,000, less ten per cent commission, for the entire property, advancing the price as in their discretion warranted by the disclosure of greater volume or values."

That same month a meeting was held in the Commercial Hotel, on Cambie Street just north of Hastings, which was then one of Vancouver's leading hotelries. Attending it were David and Leopold Boscowitz and the trapper, Oliver Furry. The point, was they told Furry, they wanted to sell the remaining three-tenths interest, but because a road was necessary to reach these claims, Furry would have to lower his interest if the necessary work was to be done and the property sold.

The recommendation to sell was approved, and an approach was made to C.J. Valentine, an English capitalist, in August 1900. The Englishman took a bond on the property for $750,000, but before it could be executed, he insisted on having a London mining engineer, J.D. Kendall, examine the property. He also insisted that, if the glowing report of the owners did not stand up, they would have to pay all expenses. Kendall's reports were, of course, favorable and the first two payments of $5000 each were made, but then Valentine died and the executors of the estate decided to back out of the picture.

The Syndicate was finding, that though they had what had been described several times as a "mountain of ore", the obstacles which lay ahead, largely financial, were going to be difficult to overcome. In August 1901, after several other attempts had been made to sell the property, George H. Robinson, of Butte, Montana, appeared with an offer. The financial state of the Syndicate was put bluntly in a minute of the board for August 9: "it was made an incidental condition that he (Robinson) furnish the funds necessary to payment of the existing liabilities…to meet which we have no funds."

That fall Robinson purchased the ten shares in the Syndicate held by Walters at $1500 a share, thus obtaining a controlling interest in the mine. In June 1903 he bought out the Boscowitz for $53,000, obtaining the Fairview, Edith Fraction, Jane Clifton, Mineral Creek, William and Heather Fractions, which were bought into the Syndicate.

Robinson immediately set to work reorganizing the Syndicate, increasing its capitalization and establishing a new board of directors. This board consisted of the Hon. Edgar Dewdney, president; C.W. McMeekin, vice-president; G.H. Robinson, managing director; J.W. Lee, secretary; H.C. Bellinger of Butte and C.M. Dull as directors.

President Dewdney was one of the moulders of British Columbia and the Canadian west. A Devon man, he came to British Columbia in 1859, the year after gold was discovered on the Fraser. He was 24 years of age and had qualified as a civil engineer.

On his arrival in Victoria he found employment under Governor James Douglas and Colonel R.C. Moody, commanding officer of the Royal Engineers garrison and chief commissioner of lands and works. The first task assigned to him was the laying out of the infant capital of the colony, New Westminster. In 1860 he began construction of a trail through the mountains from Hope to the Kootenays which became known as the Dewdney Trail which roughly corresponds today with the Southern Trans-provincial Highway. In 1869 Dewdney was elected to the colonial council, representing Kootenay and when British Columbia entered the Canadian Confederation in 1871 he represented the area in the House of Commons in Ottawa where he sat as a Conservative, a follower of Sir John A. Macdonald.

In 1879 Dewdney was made Indian commissioner and in 1881 lieutenant-governor of the Northwest Territories, then the practically uninhabited central part of Canada, containing the present provinces of Alberta, Saskatchewan and part of Manitoba. During his administration the Metis, or halfbreed followers of Louis Riel rose up in rebellion and it was largely due to Dewdney's efforts that the Indians as a whole didn't join the revolt. In 1888 he entered Sir John's cabinet as minister of the interior, a post he held until 1892 when he was named lieutenant-governor of British Columbia, being in office until 1897.

The new stock of the Syndicate was underwritten by Henry Stern of New York, and he in turn interested in the financing of the enterprise Grant Barney Schley of the banking firm of Moore and Schley. Schley had had wide experience in mining affairs in United States and in Mexico and he was to take a deep personal interest in the affairs of the Britannia property.

On taking over the management of the property Robinson launched an extensive development program, making a raise from the former tunnel to the surface in the Mammoth Bluff and opening it up as a glory hole. He installed a Riblet aerial tramway, three and four-fifths miles in length, which cost $75,000. Buildings were erected for a plant, a concentrating mill was installed and a production of 200 tons a day was attained, although plans were adopted to increase it to 400 tons a day.

The upper terminal of the tramway was connected with the Jane and Mammoth Bluff mines by tramways of 600 and 700 feet respectively, built on trestles. At the upper terminal a Sturtevant crusher was installed, driven by a 30 h.p. induction motor. The crushed ore traversed a sorting belt where waste rock was picked out and thrown on the waste dump, while the ore was delivered to a bin with a capacity of 1000 tons. A 12-drill Rand compressor was installed and operated by electric power which was developed from a hydro plant on Britannia Creek. The mill included a Blake rock crusher, two Gates rolls, a Hancock jig, two Huntington and two Chilean mills. The concentration plant had two Camett tables, 11 Wifley tables, 12 Overstrom tables, 38 Frue vanners and tow Sperry slimers. The power plant had two four-foot Pelton wheels, two Westinghouse AC 200 k.w. generators, one 40 k.w. and two small direct current generators and seven induction motors. An electric railway connecting the docks with the mill was installed, operated by a Baldwin Westinghouse mine locomotive.

In 1903 the *Report of the Minister of Mines* for British Columbia showed that the townsite, covering 150 acres, was "partially cleared." On November 1, 1904, W. Fleet Robertson, the provincial mineralogist, visited the property and found in process of construction "what promises to be one of the largest concentrating plants in B.C., the completion of which must have a powerful influence upon the mining development of this section of the province. Robertson noted a "substantial dock" had been built, a "commodious office, quarters for the officers" a store, and several private homes. George W. Campbell had been given a lease on company property, for $5 a year, on which to build a hotel. The concentrator, Robinson said, was "a large rectangular building built upon piles at the water's edge" and about a hundred yards distant, work had started on a 500 ton crushing plant.

Meanwhile Henry Stern had incorporated, under the laws of the state of Maine, a new company, the Howe Sound Company, with a capital of $2 million, divided into shares of $5 par. On April 8, 1904 an extraordinary general meeting of the Syndicate was held in the Fairfield Building in Vancouver to hear Stern's proposals. Henry

Stern was there in person, and the following summary was entered into the minute book.

"Mr. Stern's proposal is that in exchange for the shares of the Britannia Copper Syndicate he will deliver $1,000,000 in shares of the Howe Sound Company fully paid for distribution among the shareholders of the Britannia Syndicate, each share of the Britannia Syndicate being entitled to 500 shares of the Howe Sound Company. In addition Mr. Stern undertakes to provide $225,000 in cash in exchange for $500,000 in shares of the Howe Sound Company, and to undertake that the additional $500,000 in stock in the Howe Sound Company shall not be sold or disposed of except with the sanction of the Board of Directors of the Britannia Copper Syndicate, and then only for the purposes of the Britannia Copper Syndicate properties, and that the said shares will be held by the financial agents of the Britannia Copper Syndicate to be appointed in the City of New York.

"In addition," the minute book entry continues, "Mr. Stern offers that every present shareholder of the Britannia Copper Syndicate shall be entitled as a matter of right within thirty days from the passage of any resolution made on this proposal to elect to take his pro-rata shares of the said $500,000 in shares in which he is to receive from the $225,000 in cash, so that each shareholder of the Company shall be entitled to share in the subscription the same as the said Henry Stern and that the said Henry Stern will take either the whole of the said $500,000 in shares or any less proportion which may not be subscribed by the shareholders. The $225,000 to be paid over by the said Stern to the financial agents of the Britannia Copper Syndicate at the City of New York subject to the order of the Board of Directors and to be used only for the purposes of the Company in equipment and development of the Company's properties. The total sum of $225,000 to be paid from time to time as required and within nine months from date in any event."

The stockholders meeting voted unanimously in favor of the Stern proposition, and after the meeting, Edgar Dewdney met the press and told them "It is settled that we shall proceed energetically with the work of development and equipment of the camp."

To this date no ore had been shipped from the Britannia mine, and in mining circles there was much speculation as to where the output would be sent for smelting. Most commonly mentioned smelter was Crofton, on Vancouver which came into existence in 1901 when

Henry Croft, brother-in-law of James Dunsmuir, the island coal and railway baron, purchased acreage on Osborne Bay for a smelter and townsite. The following year a bond issue on the Northwestern Smelting and Refining Company was floated. Construction got underway under the direction of Herman C. Bellinger and J. Breen of Butte, Montana. Both these men had been involved in the building of the Northport, Idaho and Trail smelters. The Crofton smelter was fired up in September 1902 to process ores from the Lenora mine on nearby Mount Sicker.

Speculation as to the smelter ended on May 6, 1905 when the Syndicate met in the law offices of Davis, Marshall and McNeill to hear another proposition from George H. Robinson. This was "to sell the Company the Crofton smelter and a half interest in certain portions of the Townsite of Crofton." To enable them to make this purchase a new company was formed, the Britannia Limited, which agreed to the purchase.

The townsite in which the Britannia company acquired an interest was quite a town. It had a post office, two general stores, a butcher shop, hardware store, community hall and two hotels. One of these catered to the "refined" taste and the other suited what was described as the "sporting crowd". A stake of $1000 in a card game was not exceptional and both hotels had ample provisions in stock for moistening the throats of thirsty mining men. The doors swung in and the doors swung out for 24 hours a day. Drinking, playing cards and bar-room brawling, however, were only a part of Crofton's life. Concerts and plays were put on and some of the "refined" members of the community hosted private champagne parties.

With the Syndicate, the smelting company came under the control of the Howe Sound Company which also held interests in the El Potosi Mining Company, of Chihuahua and Calera Mining Company, both in Mexico.

On the same day that the Britannia Smelting Company was formed the syndicate voted to move their registered offices from Vancouver to Britannia Beach.

Behind the scenes the Boscowitz' had been proving to be a bit of a headache. Thomas Turner was fighting them, the Syndicate was fighting them, and caught up in the middle of the battle was the trapper Oliver Furry. It all went back to the original deal between the

Boscowitz family and Oliver Furry when the question arose as to whether the rubber stamp signature "Boscowitz & Son" on the agreement was legal. If it wasn't one of the parties was out of the picture, and the Boscowitz' were too worldly to allow it to happen to them. Secondly, if the original was legal, did Furry sign the second agreement which reduced his interested from 50 per cent to 20 per cent. There were other complexities which had to be answered and these proved too much for this illiterate trapper from McNab Creek. In 1905, driven insane by worry and confusion, Oliver Furry was committed to the mental asylum in New Westminster where, that same year, he died.

In the fall of 1906 Charles McMeekin, on behalf of the Syndicate, took the case to court. Oliver's interest was represented by his brother, Ira, who for his legal council had Joseph Martin, KC, the same "Fightin' Joe" who, for a few months in 1900 had been the tempestuous premier of British Columbia. The case was heard before Mr. Justice Hunter and was appealed to the Supreme Court in Canada. The outcome of the long and involved litigation was that the rubber stamp signature was compared to that of a "mark" and the court ruled it legal, and secondly it was decided that Furry had not signed the second document and thus held a 50 per cent interest.

Donkey engine on the incline, about 1914. BMM #12934

Whipsawing lumber at the Utopia Dam, 1914. BMM #10885

Aerial tramway, 1912. BMM #11507

Building the incline, 1914. BMM #13907

Britannia Beach from the powerhouse, 1915. BMM #11508

Tram transfer station, Halfway Camp, 1915. BMM #12948

Jane Camp, 1914. BMM #12868

3

A DICTATOR IN CAMP

A note of sadness entered into the minutes of the Britannia Smelting Company held on July 6, 1906. Two days before George Robinson, the man who had done so much to put the mine into production had died. The meeting desired "at this the first meeting after receipt of the sad intelligence to have spread upon the record of their proceedings that it is with the deepest sorrow and regret that they learn of the loss of one who has always taken such a prominent and loyal interest in the affairs of the company."

The future of the company now lay in the hands of G.B. Schley of New York. Would the project be abandoned and all the investment lost, or would it continue? Schley, who had a large map of the property pinned to his office wall, had followed with keen interest the development work thus far carried on, and although he was thousands of miles away from the mine site, he "knew" the property intimately and he was enough of a visionary to realize the immense potential of the Britannia Mine. Thus he ordered the work to continue.

A further step in the corporate development of the company was taken on September 1, 1908 with the formation of the Britannia Mining and Smelting Company Limited, organized under the laws of British Columbia. It took over the assets of the Britannia Copper

Syndicate and the Britannia Smelting Company, while still being a subsidiary company to the Howe Sound Company. Charles Dull succeeded Robinson, and in a very short time Dull was succeeded by Mason T. Adams. Dewdney was elected president of the new company and R.H. Leach became vice-president and general manager; Y.M. White, secretary-treasurer and D.G. Marshall and C.B. McNeill directors.

Under Leach's direction one of the lower working tunnels was driven in to crosscut a vein, the outcrop of which was exposed on the mountain top. This outcrop was not very promising but it contained much less iron and zinc than the deposits which up to that time had been opened up. For the next two years a force of between 150 and 200 men developed this vein along with several others, but as the provincial mineralogist, W. Fleet Robertson pointed out in the 1911 *Report of the Minister of Mines*, "little is heard about the Britannia mine and it is realized by but a few how much work is going on there very quietly."

"The camp," he wrote, "does not advertise itself and its stock is not usually dealt in on the exchanges, yet the property employed, during 1911, an average of 145 men below ground and 180 men above ground and mined about 500 tons of ore a working day."

Leach's health gave out in 1911 forcing him to give up his post, and on November 22, 1911 a successor was appointed. He was a big, tough, unsmiling mining man who was as colorful in himself as was his name, John Wedderburn Dunbar Moodie.

The board of directors named him vice-president and general manager, but above and beyond these positions, he was Barney Schley's man and of that there was no doubt in anyone's mind.

On his arrival in camp a long deep tunnel was started 1200 feet lower than the old one beginning half-way up the tram line, near the "transfer station". To reach this new scene of operations, Moodie built a surface electric tramway, and also under his direction work got underway on a new storage dam as well as a concentrator which was to be the largest in the province.

During Moodie's first year at Britannia the labor force was increased to between 650 and 700 men and an auxiliary steam plant was erected at the Beach, along with a large number of cottages and an up-to-date hospital. The Mining Report for 1912 says a large store was in course of construction "and the company's aim is to have everything needed on the ground for the employees benefit."

The store, near the site of the present "Met" building, was a three storey department store, which indeed, carried everything needed, but its public relations needed a stiff shot in the arm. The residents of the Beach thought prices "outrageous", but what particularly rankled them was that they were not permitted to buy anything from the "outside". Thus the Woodwards, Eatons and Spencer's catalogues were like forbidden fruit; to be admired but not touched. One employee had a brother who was a foreman at Pat Burns packing house in Vancouver, and while in the city the miner was given a ham which he put into his suitcase. As ill-luck would have it, as he stepped off the boat at Britannia, the suitcase flew open and out rolled the ham and Moodie saw it. Despite the protestations that it was a gift, Moodie wouldn't believe him. "You can't tell me you got that ham for nothing," he is reported to have said, "Pack up and get back to town."

"Pack up and get back to town" seems to have been a common phrase in the mine in those days. If you disputed a bill at the store, the debate often ended with "if you don't like it, pack up and get back to town."

During Moodie's regime, the first attempts to organize a union at Britannia took place. This was attempted by the Industrial Workers of the World, the I.W.W., but known more familiarly as the "Wobblies". To those who showed interest in the movement Moodie had but one phrase, "Pack up and get back to town."

If Moodie didn't like something, out it went, and there were two things at Britannia Beach which J.W.D. Moodie didn't like. First there was the "temple of Bacchus" in the hotel, a room fitted with a long mahogany bar, and as per style, a large glass mirror. Moodie did not approach it with an axe and smash it up as Carrie Nation might have done, but his technique was just as effective. He ordered it closed, and when Moodie ordered something there was no argument. He converted the premises into a billiard room.

Then there was the little house on the hill, located on the old Daisy trail. Colonel Robert Tecumseh Lowery, editor of a string of sprightly mining newspapers in the Kootenay, would have said this house had red curtains hanging in the windows. It was a well-built two-storey log structure which housed four "soiled doves", a manageress of considerable physical proportions and a bouncer who was highly skilled at his profession. There was no exchange of pleasantries when the day of reckoning with Moodie arrived. Even the bouncer trembled before the power and authority of the general manager's famed words, "Pack up and get back to town." The building, incidentally, was torn down in 1931 after having served as a Japanese bunkhouse.

Thus did temperance arrive, the Wobblies leave, and the reign of the Cyprian goddesses come to an end. Henceforth Moodie would stand for no booze, no unions, and no ladies of the half-world. If a man brought liquor into camp he had to leave it at the wharf, or be content with the amount inside him – and heaven help him if Moodie found him drunk.

It is perfectly true that John Wedderburn Moodie ruled Britannia with an iron hand, but it is equally true that it was through him that the mine prospered, even though some of his techniques, to say the least, were a bit unorthodox. One of his pet theories was that the aerial tramway could be self-dumping. His idea was that if the buckets could be made to hit a certain point at a certain angle, the contents would be dumped into the bins without difficulty. The trouble was human frailty. The operator of the tramline was a couple of miles from the ore dump and it was practically impossible, nay impossible, for him to control the buckets to such a degree as to hit the head of a pin. Moodie, however, insisted it could be done, and it took a lot of persuasion to show him it couldn't.

During the summer of 1913 Britannia Beach was visited by 225 delegates from the XIIth session of the International Geological Congress which was touring Canada, and Moodie was able to show them the latest in equipment: a new 200 ton mill, a mile-long double track gravity tramway with an average grade of 15 per cent, a switchback track, five miles in length, with a three per cent grade on which gasoline locomotives were used. Everything looked rosey that year, boom was in the air, and Moodie told one visitor to the Congress that Vancouver would shortly be a suburb of Britannia. One thing, however, went wrong, the price of copper took a long plunge...downwards. Across the nation the pinch recession was felt everywhere.

On February, 1912, Premier Richard McBride introduced into the British Columbia legislature a Bill calling for the construction of the

Pacific Great Eastern Railway, and by New Years Day 1914 the section between North Vancouver and Whytecliffe was in operation. Railway surveyors were not unfamiliar with Britannia as crews of Foley, Welch & Stewart, the contractors, plotted out the route from North Vancouver through to Squamish.

That winter of 1913 was a bad one. It is said that there were bread lines on the streets of Vancouver, and as for the railway, it was having trouble selling its bonds and meeting not only construction commitments, but financial ones as well. The North Vancouver-Squamish section of the line, with its estimated $100,000 a mile cost, was shelved for the time being, but so desperate was the company for funds to meet its other commitments that they persuaded the government to pay out, in advance, the promised subsidy for construction of the Howe Sound section of the line.

Although Britannia did not get its railway for more than 40 years, it did get a few improvements during the last year of world peace. Modern firefighting equipment was purchased, and electrically operated laundry plant was installed and, for the young people, a roller rink and dance hall was built at the Beach.

The future looked gloomy for the industry and as the fateful month of August 1914 drew nigh, the price of copper dropped even further. In August, operations were curtailed 50 per cent. It is said the New York office of the Howe Sound Company wired Moodie telling him to close the mine. He ignored the order and a second one came demanding in the strongest terms that the original order be complied with, and then came a third wire commending him for keeping the mine open as the price of copper had risen.

That year, at the 500 foot level of Britannia Mountain, a tunnel from the Fairview mine came into a connection with the one from the Empress, thus effecting a passage way right through the heart of the mountain. A second through-tunnel was completed two years later, in December 1916, at the 1000 level. During the second year of the war a new wharf, 120 feet long was built, a new store, additional houses and the Utopia dam at the head of Britannia Creek was completed to a height of 50 feet and a length of 340 feet. The first half of the new mill had been built, but of greater importance was the establishment of a new Tunnel Camp to replace, as "headquarters", the original Jane camp, founded by the Boscowitz' at the 1050 level.

Monday, March 22, 1915 was only three minutes old when disaster struck. At the Tunnel Camp the sudden load thrown back on the motors and generators at the power station and the slackening of the pressure on the air compressors spelled trouble somewhere up the mountainside. A check was made, first one camp, then another, to try and pin down the cause of the trouble. Camp 1050 was silent.

At that moment, 12:03 am, Monday, March 22, 1915, it had shared the same fate as did Frank, Alberta, when at 4:10 a.m., April 29, 1903, at least 66 persons were killed when the steep sides of Turtle Mountain collapsed on the Crows Nest Pass mining town of Frank. Here above Howe Sound, between 50 and 60 men, women and children died and 22 more were injured.

Men working in mines were accustomed to tragedy; a caved in stope, an early, or a delayed blast, a tramway collapsing; a thousand and one things might go wrong. These are risks, accidental or not, that the miners and their families learn to take with a shrug of the shoulders, but this one, high up at Camp 1050 was something entirely different. It was as though one of the cataclysmic forces of creation was at work again, and in a way this was so; the face of the mountain peak, pried loose by alternate seepage into a fault and then freezing hard, broke loose and started an avalanche that ploughed through the camp leaving in its wake, death, injury and devastation. It is a miracle that anybody survived, and it was a miracle that the new Tunnel Camp was spared. Only two days before the bald face of the mountain had been inspected by a team of company geologists and it appeared to these experts to be solid.

As soon as the trouble was noted at the Tunnel Camp emergency crews set up the Jane Creek draw towards the little camp. As the men trudged through the deep snow, fear was in every heart and it didn't take long to realize how close disaster had come to Tunnel Camp itself. Standing in the blackness of night, scarcely ten minutes from home, the men saw before them the 1000-foot wide swatch the slide had made down the mountainside, and they heard a voice, a voice which spoke in tones of terror and horror. And out of the darkness and into the light of flickering candles staggered a Japanese workman who blurted out, almost incoherently, the tragic story. A few minutes later the rescue party found H. Dupuis who had been picked up by the slide and rode it down the mountain, miraculously surviving the ordeal.

Two hours after the tragedy occurred the telephone rang in Provincial Police constable M.T. Spence's home at the Beach, and within minutes, one by one, candles were lit in homes and little groups began to form on the streets to discuss the tragedy and organize relief work. Spence lost no time in heading up the trail towards Tunnel Camp, and with him were James Drysburgh, Donald McDonald and Dr. W. F. Dudley, the camp medical officer. And at Tunnel Camp every available man had rushed to the scene. When the Beach party arrived a large gang of men were digging out the dead and injured the best way they could, utilizing the feeble light of mine candles.

Later that night an exhausted Constable Spence told newsmen who had rushed up from Vancouver, "I found that the mine office, store, rock crusher, tram terminus, a big bunk house and a half dozen homes had been blotted out by the millions of tons of rock, mud and snow, which in some places was piled 50 feet deep over what had been the level of the camp. Also destroyed that night was Cotto Damton's school house near the mouth of the mine, and he was amongst the missing."

"The cookhouse," said *The Vancouver Sun*, the next day "lies beneath a small ugly hill of rock and earth which completely obliterated it."

All food and provisions had been carried away and now the Herculean task of packing, on the backs of men, vast quantities of goods, shovels and medical supplies.

News of the disaster did not reach Vancouver until mid-morning when an almost exhausted man arrived by rowboat at Horseshoe Bay and called the authorities to make an appeal for doctors and nurses. He did not know the details of the mountain tragedy, only that there had been a terrible accident.

At 11 a.m. Dr. R.E. McKechnie, Dr. George Clement and a Dr. Simpson were enroute to Britannia on the SS *Ballena*. Accompanying them were nurses Lillian Turnbull, M.J. Mobbs, Mrs. Scribner and Miss Rhodes. Vancouver police chief Malcolm B. MacLennan offered the police launch *PML No. 1* to the Provincial Police and 20 minutes after the offer was made Sergeant George Hood, Constable Samuel North, J.C. Moss and Sid Saunders were on their way. Accompanying them was Bruce A. "Pinkie" McKelvie, of *The*

Vancouver Province editorial staff, years later to be acclaimed British Columbia's leading historical writer.

"It is impossible to convey on paper the awfulness of the tragedy," McKelvie wrote. "The residents of the camp here do not realize the full significance of the catastrophe. They are stunned and dazed by its terrible suddenness and have not yet had time to grasp the enormity of the disaster. Every person is engaged in some task. Women are making bandages, while those men who are not up the mountain at work digging for bodies are constructing coffins or preparing supplies. The company's great department store here has been a hive of activity ever since the first news of the disaster was received and not only has Mr. Donahue been busy directing the work, but Mr. Miller, the post master, has been engaged in getting out casualty lists and sending out tidings over the wire to anxious relatives."

Then came the eye-witness accounts, but they were few. Most of the survivors were too shocked and stunned by the disaster to talk about it.

Henry Baxter, asleep in Bunkhouse No. 3 had been awakened by a shock of such force he thought the power house at the 800 foot level had been blown up.

"It was pitch dark," Baxter said, "I turned on a light and it flicked out right away. I told the fellows it could not be the magazine because the windows were not broken. I had no idea what had happened. Pretty soon we began to hear shouts for help. We got into our clothes and some of us didn't. We went out in the dark and didn't know what to do. Pretty soon it seemed like the whole camp was groaning and calling for help, and to bring a light and for God's sake somebody come here quick. We ran around and tried to do something. But there was no light to see by at first. We got candles and lanterns; but what good could we do? Only a little. Some of the hurt men crawled along the ground and some were able to walk.

"Everybody was hollering and nobody could do much. But we did the best we could. I don't want to see anything like it again as long as I live. It's awful to hear a big man groan when he's hurt. As soon as it got light we could do better. We got a lot of badly hurt men out and some dead men, too. We got out one mucker who was killed with two of his babies, while his wife and the smallest baby wasn't hurt. You ought to see where the diningroom was. It's a pile of rocks as big as a ship. You can't see the house."

The home of foreman Thomas McCullough, or McCulla, his wife and child was "buried so deeply that the spot where it stood is unrecognizable and the house cannot be seen." McCullough was just inside the mouth of the mine checking off the out-going shift, when the slide occurred. He was almost buried, but although bruised and bleeding, he managed to extricate himself.

One of the saddest cases was that of a Mrs. Appleton and her two children. She had recently given birth to a child and that morning had brought the baby up to the mine. She and the children were killed but the husband survived.

Mrs. A.W. Owen, whose house was near the big crusher, said "the slide smashed the crusher like it crushed ore from the mine." Several Japanese workmen were smashed with it. Mrs. Owen heard their "pitiful moans for help and their ceaseless groaning with the agony of their suffering."

"I thought," she said later, "it was a hurricane. You've heard a big wind when it tears down trees and it thunders and lightning crashes. It was just like that. The lights went out. I could hear terrible moaning. The children call me Muzzie and that is what my husband calls at night when he comes to the door. When I realized that something terrible had happened and heard the groans I was certain my husband was moaning "Muzzie". I lighted the candles and put them in the windows I peered out into the black night. Of course there was nothing to see, it was a very black and the air was full of strange sounds and close to the house I could hear the Japanese moan. My husband was on his way home and soon arrived."

C.E. Copeland, of Seattle, a young mining engineer who had just refused an appointment as professor geology in an eastern university because he wanted to stay in the field, was killed along with his bride of a few months.

The majority of the casualties occurred in Bunkhouse No. 1. Three men were sitting on the side of the bunk. Two were killed, while the man in the middle was carried away by the force of the slide. Another man in that bunkhouse was picked up and rolled with the snow. When found he was hard-packed in a snowball, only his head and one hand being out.

Three young men, C.F. Morse, Stanley Park and C. Perry were lodging in the company's office building when the disaster struck. The slide sliced off the roof and hurled them through the open top into the night. These three men woke W.A. Wylie, the mine superintendent who apparently had slept through all the disturbance. Piled up against the corner of his house was a wall of debris. With "bugs" they stumbled over the sea of mud until they met some other men who were sent to the mine for shovels and candles. "We could hear a cry," Wylie said, "and would search in that direction until we could locate the place where the cry came from and then we would remove the debris from the poor fellow."

With great difficulty the bodies of the victims were brought down the mountain trail to Britannia where, on Wednesday, March 24, coroner C.E. Jeffs held an inquest.

"Many touching scenes were witnessed as the rough boxes containing the mangled dead were placed on board the boat," said *The Province*. "As the *Ballena* pulled away from the wharf and Captain Cates dropped her flag to half mast, every man on the deck lifted his hat and stood uncovered taking a last silent farewell to his comrades and companions." The *Ballena* carried 26 bodies and one of the injured, an Italian, Ernie Campanolla, who was in very serious condition with a badly crushed chest and shoulders.

That night two thousand people packed every available foot of space at the Terminal Steam Navigation Company's dock at the foot of Carrall Street in Vancouver to watch, silently, as the *Ballena*, her flag still at half mast, steamed slowly into her berth.

"In silence the boat tied up," wrote the Province reporter on the scene, "and the first rough-boarded casket with its freight of dead was moved forward onto the dock. Reverently every head was bared and here and there a woman was heard to quietly sob. A passageway was made through the crowd of Sgt. Munro and some of his policeman and the passengers who accompanied the funeral ship, mostly relatives of the dead, passed through the crowd. Words of sympathy and condolence were whispered and were responded to by silent but eloquent hand-clasps.

"Meanwhile the work of removing the coffins to the storehouse on the wharf was soon concluded. Dead wagons were outside the gates waiting. These soon commenced the work of removing the remains of the dead from the little mountain mining camp to the various morgues to which they had been assigned."

Back at Britannia the grim search for survivors went on and hopes died hard.

Half a century later, the scars of that terrible March night remain on the face of the mountain and in the minds of those who were in camp that night.

The aftermath of the Jane Slide. BMM #13163

Upper tram terminal at the Jane Basin, 1050 level, 1915.
BMM #13165

Pack train with supplies to build Park Lane and Utopia dams on
Upper Britannia Creek, 1915. BMM #14022

The Townsite, or later Mount Sheer, in the making. BMM #11266

No. 2 Mill. BMM #13542

No. 2 Mill after the fire of 1921. BMM #11529

No. 2 Mill after the fire of 1921. BMM #13988

The Beach Hotel, 1920. BMM #13688

Britannia Creek, flowing through Britannia Beach in 1919.
BMM #11516

Original "high level" bridge, taken out in 1921 flood and replaced with steel span. BMM #11269

Britannia Beach before the flood. BMM #12989

4

FIRE AND FLOOD

The disaster at the 1050 Camp was followed a month later by news of the great battle of St. Julien in France where the First Canadian Division, including the Duke of Connaught's Own Rifles of Vancouver, won their battle honors.

All across Canada communities large and small were engaged in making and sending comforts to the boys overseas and Britannia Beach and the Tunnel Townsite were no exceptions. It is not recorded how many pairs of woollen socks, scarves and mitts were turned out by the ladies in the twin Howe Sound communities, nor is it recorded how many parcels were sent to the trenches, but a company report states they were "amongst the most active communities in Canada in war work" not only in sending the packages overseas but in supporting the various patriotic fund drives. One of the projects launched by the mine employees was the raising of $2500 which provided the 72nd Regiment, Seaforth Highlanders of Vancouver with machine guns. These were marked and named "Britannia Machine Gun No. 1" and "Britannia Machine Gun No. 2".

As far as the mine was concerned more troubles lurked, though of a minor note when compared to the 1050 disaster. During September, October and November there was a drought which forced the suspension of operations. However in 1916 the mill went into full production under the control of the Imperial Munitions Board. Record production figures were reached and subsequently passed as the mill worked to capacity. Not only were the miners and production people kept busy, but so were the small army of carpenters and tradesmen. The Tunnel Townsite, in later years called Mt. Sheer Townsite, begun in 1914, was now taking on all the aspects of a fair-sized town. In 1916 a school was built, as was a hospital with a three bed ward, operating room, dispensary and nurses' quarters. Other buildings erected were an engineering office, a three storey recreation building containing a billiard room, barber shop, general reading room and dance hall which could easily be converted into a motion picture theatre.

Down at the Beach, a general office building and motion picture theatre was built, while at the 500-foot level on the south side of Britannia Mountain, a new camp, known as the Barbara, was opened. It is quite likely that the Barbara owes its name to Barbara Boscowitz. This little alpine village was not as isolated as it might seem, for a tunnel connected it with the Tunnel Townsite. Here, at the Barbara, accommodation was arranged for 80 men in two bunkhouses which were supplied with hot and cold running water.

In March 1917 the camp was saddened by the news of the death of their president, the Honourable Edgar Dewdney, a man who it was noted in the minutes of the directors' meeting on March 5, "has long been connected with the Company and who has always been held in the highest esteem by all officers and employees." In his place, Grant B. Schley, of New York, was elected President.

A year later, almost to this day, the directors noted in their minutes: "It is with feelings of the deepest regret that we mourn the loss of our President, Grant B. Schley, whose passing away removes from our midst one to whom this Company is indebted beyond expression. His judgment, courage and financial support are responsible for the present status of this Company."

He had insisted on expending large amounts of money monthly on development work, often contrary to the advice of technical advisors.

As successor, E.B. Schley was named president, and that year, C.P. Browning, who had been associated with the company since 1914, was appointed general superintendent.

The great news for 1918, of course, was the end of the war. When the news reached the Beach a great celebration ensued, with a snake parade around town and down to the mine manager's house, but Moodie, despite the gaiety and the great occasion being celebrated, refused to make an appearance on his front porch, and few people in camp realized the tragedy which had struck the Moodie household. Down in Vancouver, the 'flu' epidemic was raging unchecked and one of the victims was Moodie's daughter, Fannie, a student at Crofton House School. Thus his reluctance to acknowledge the employees' demonstration becomes understandable. So far, Britannia had escaped the deadly virus, but just as the fogs blanketed Howe Sound and Britannia so you could hardly see ten feet ahead, so did the 'flu' blanket the Beach and very little anybody could do about it. For weeks there was practically no work done in the mines. Men died like flies in the bunkhouses, and the dance hall up at the Townsite became a temporary hospital. At the Beach, Dr. Roberts, the camp medical officer, had his hands full. The hospital was full, every house had somebody sick in it, and his task was made even more difficult when the nurse up at the Townsite succumbed to the ravages of 'flu'. The best the doctor could do was to give the men plenty of whisky and hope for the best. At the Townsite, Bob Ryan, a first aid man, took over the job of nursing the camp back to health, and at the Beach, Yip Bing, the Chinese boy who worked in the store, made and delivered on his little wagon, pots and pots of soup, earning for himself the title "Doctor Y.B".

At night, the aerial tramway became a funeral cortege as bodies, sometimes as many as a dozen at a time, were brought down to await the steamer for Vancouver. It is not known how many died during the 'flu' epidemic at Britannia, but estimates range all the way from 40 to over the hundred mark.

The 'flu' was only one of Moodie's problems as the mine prepared to celebrate its first peacetime Christmas in four years. Now that Kaiser Wilhelm II had become the lowly woodchopper of Doorn, the question arose: What was the future of the copper industry? It didn't take too long for the bad news to be known.

While the copper industry throughout North America was worrying about their future, life had to go on. In 1919 the old concentrator and vanner building was torn down and on its site a two storey recreation hallway was built at the Beach. The *Report of the*

Minister of Mines states it was 72-feet long by 30-feet wide and contained a billiard hall "furnished with an English billiard table and three pool tables."

It had long been felt that, successful as the mine had been, it was a sort of plaything for Grant B. Schley, and when the copper market began to show definite signs of hardening, the time had come for a tightening up of the operations. As a result J.W.D. Moodie left and returned to the United States (where he subsequently married Schley's housekeeper). His resignation was accepted by the board on August 7, 1920, and B.B. Nieding was elected general manager. Nieding, however, lasted less than a month, and on August 30, 1920, answering the call of a better position elsewhere, he resigned and was succeeded by E.J. Donohue.

In the cold, black and white of the printed page, J.W.D. Moodie may seem to emerge as a man devoid of the milk of human kindness. The records speak of only the visible man and not what lay beneath this creature of sorrows. He deserves a defence and an understanding.

Friendship never came easy to him, nor did laughter or gaiety, his background did not permit it. The son of a prominent Hamilton, (Ont.) family, Moodie Underwear, he grew up in what might be described as an unhappy environment. He was not allowed to play with other children because he was told they were not good enough for him. All through life he was a "loner", never able to be really at ease with others. The few friends he made at Britannia, and these were on the executive level only, are quick to point out that when he did make a friend he was a devoted friend who could rise to any occasion. To his family, who resided in the Big House down by the waterfront, he was a devoted husband and father, but tragedy stalked through his household. About 1915 his wife gave birth to a child at the Britannia hospital, but it did not live for very long, and shortly afterwards, Mrs. Moodie herself passed away. As we have seen, his daughter succumbed to the 'flu'. Moodie and his son, Robert, bore the grief alone.

By the time Moodie resigned the bottom had fallen out of the copper market. Where copper had been selling on the New York market for 20 cents a pound it dropped to 14 cents. As a result in November 1920, production was temporarily discontinued, the concentrator and incline tramway, as well as the electric railway, were closed down and the payroll was reduced by 40 per cent.

"The results, until production is resumed," noted the Mines Department report for 1921 "are serious, especially when the fact is considered that the tonnage of ore mined (at Britannia) under normal conditions is about 2500 tons each day, and the number of employees on the payroll is about 1000."

Luckily, this black cloud had a golden lining to it. Despite the drop in the price of copper the mine was at least open, thanks to the silver and gold in the ore and the fact that the directors put their trust in the results of an exploration and development program.

Hard hit as Britannia was, it came off easily by comparison to other copper centres in British Columbia. In the Boundary district, in the southern interior, the effects of the slump were disastrous. The mines around the city of Phoenix, such great producers as Old Ironside, Knobb Hill, Gold Drop, Brooklyn, Stemwinder, Mother Lode, Deadwood, and others shut down completely. The fires in the smelters at Greenwood, Boundary Falls and Grand Forks were extinguished, never to be started up again. And Phoenix, a "big brassy place full of locomotives, blasting, four churches, champion hockey teams, 8 saloons, five dance halls, gambling casinos, the biggest plate glass windows in the west, and a boarding house where 400 miners once had a fight over a girl," was allowed to die. And so was the little community of Anaconda, a residential district just south of the Greenwood smelter. Copper Mountain and Allenby closed up shop, as did Anyox in the far north.

On June 23, 1921 "a site for a mining camp on Furry Creek was selected in the virgin forest near the portal of the Victoria crosscut audit on the 1800 foot level." The *Report of the Minister of Mines* noted that a sawmill with a capacity of 20,000 BM, designed to handle the cutting and shaping of mine timbers, had been installed and two bunkhouses, one for the white miners and the other for the Japanese, had been erected. In addition, two dining rooms "and all other necessary building to accommodate 100 employees had been built."

The hopes of the directors received two serious setbacks in 1921. On the night of March 7 the concentrator burned down in a fire with mysterious origins. It began in the crusher, and the draft created by the blaze sent the flames racing through the whole mountainside building. At the Beach the fire siren screamed and all available men rushed to the scene. E.J. Donohue realized from the outset that it was hopeless to try to save the concentrator but every effort must be made to prevent the fire from spreading to the nearby power house, which fortunately, was done. Nobody was injured in the blaze, but without the concentrator, it was impossible to carry on mining activity.

Almost immediately the firm of Bradley, Bruff & Labarthe, of San Francisco began the task of building Britannia's third concentrator. This time it was built of steel and concrete and was "absolutely fireproof".

The second blow began with a strange series of events. On October 19 two miners, L.C. Craig and Francis Patenaude became trapped in the mine and for the next eight days the question on everybody's lips was: "Are they dead or alive?"

"It was on that note," the *Vancouver Sun* stated, "that the town was divided – the patient, tearful wives of the men clinging to the hope that their loved ones would be found alive, with assurance from officials of the company, while hardened old miners of years of service expected only the bodies of their comrades to be found."

"Sparing no effort or expense in the rescue work," the *Sun* continued, "the Britannia company brought in all of its most experienced miners from the Tunnel and Victoria camps to assist the local rescue gangs in the stern task of boring through 40-feet of water-soaked earth and rock, with water pouring into the emergency shaft, turning the debris into muck, the rescuers worked knee deep in the churning mass of rock and earth wet to the skin."

The rescue work was hampered by the fear that the picks of the relief party, breaking into the safety room where the men were believed to be trapped, might cause a further cave-in. Finally, eight days later, on October 27, Jim and Tom Curnow reached the entombed men and minutes later the shout went up "They are alive!"

The men were suffering from hunger and exposure, but otherwise seemed to be in good shape after their ordeal and were quickly rushed to the hospital at the Beach for treatment.

That night, even though rain had been pelting down for the past few days, a sort of carnival atmosphere took over both the Beach and the Tunnel camps, despite the fact that earlier in the day a miner, by the name of Basil Dorner, had been killed in an accident and his body had been brought down to the Beach awaiting the steamer for Vancouver. The next day was Sunday, and Father J. B. McDonald of

St. Helen's Roman Catholic Church, Vancouver, who had come up to Britannia to administer if necessary, the Last Rites to Patenaude, celebrated Mass in one of the private homes. Prayers were said in thanksgiving for the mine rescue, and for the protection of the people of Squamish, Pitt Meadows and Port Coquitlam which were being badly battered by flood waters.

More than 7 to 8 miles behind Britannia Beach, extra watchmen were on duty at the three dams used to provide water power for the mine, and the village felt secure that the fate which had taken over the three other communities would not befall them. But halfway between the dams and the beach, apparently unknown to the watchmen, a lake, many acres in extent, was rapidly building up behind a natural driftwood dam. Shortly before 9 p.m., Sunday night, this dam broke and in two minutes 37 persons were dead and 15 others seriously injured.

At that moment Jim Emmott and Bert King were standing close to the point where Britannia Creek enters the town and were thus, in all probability, the first to see the roaring wall of water descend upon the darkened community. Both turned and started running into town shouting warnings which the sound of the rushing water drowned almost before it left their lips. Before they could go many yards the water was on top of them. By one of those queer tricks of fate, King was thrown clear by the rampaging waters and was picked up later with a badly crushed leg and other injuries, but Emmott was swept away and his body was later recovered from the waters of Howe Sound.

William Lonon, a watchman and one of the oldest employees of the company, who had won praise for his actions in fighting the concentrator fire earlier in the year, had just completed his first evening inspection and was warming himself in the boiler room of the machinery buildings. Suddenly the terrifying roar which heralded the coming of the death wave reached his ears and he rushed out into the night.

"With the waters bearing down on him," said *the Province*, "and the prospect of instant death staring him in the face, Lonon did not hesitate for a second. He dashed down the main-street shrieking a warning and met heroic death doing his duty when the flood overwhelmed the town."

Miss Elaine Peterson, the "hello-girl", was alone in the compressor telephone exchange when at 9:30 she received a message, "For God's sake warn everybody to get out of their houses!" She relayed the message to as many as possible.

The camp medical officer, Dr. A.M. Menzies, was standing in the centre of the street leading down to the wharf and was hurled against a post by the force of the flood. Nearly drowned and badly bruised, the doctor clung to the post for dear life until rescued, and within half an hour, was ministering to the injured and dying.

Another hero that night was Bert Bacon, of the Dominion Government customs office. A holder of a Royal Humane Society medal and the Military Medal, he lived in a house just clear of the path of the flood. When he heard the roar from the mountain gorge above town he rushed out into the night to see the homes of friends wiped out right before his very eyes. On a piece of wreckage Bacon noticed a tiny baby and plunged into the water to rescue it. He succeeded in reaching the child but was almost carried to death himself. After a struggle he managed to grasp a piece of clothes line, which fortunately held, and using this he brought himself and his precious bundle to safety.

Mr. and Mrs. George Peterson that awful night were at home when the torrent swept through town. Their home was situated right in the path of the flood and it was swept away before they had time to step to the front door. They climbed into the attic when they found escape impossible and breaking through a window, Mr. Peterson went out onto the roof to find the house already floating some 50 feet out in Howe Sound. His cries for help attracted the attention of a rescue party who sent out a boat to bring the family to safety.

Mr. and Mrs. Aleck Anderson, too, had a fortunate escape when their home was carried away. It was one of a whole line of company houses that was carried down towards the general store. Both occupants made a dash for the front door to find that the flood was so rapid that certain death would result from any attempt to escape. They tried another entrance but that too was of no use. Finally, when the house bumped against another dwelling place near the hotel they made their escape.

Miss Murphy, the school teacher, was rescued with difficulty from a window as her home floated with the current down to Howe Sound.

It was a night for heroism, and everyone who experienced those frightening hours, had a story to tell, and one of those unselfish acts which are still remembered is the bravery of Yip Bing, the Chinese boy who worked in the company store. Nearby was the home of store manager Archie Mathiesen which stood right in the path of the wall of water. It was swept off its foundations and was carried by the water for more than two city blocks before being smashed to matchwood between huge boulders and floating logs. As it went giddily by, Bing, somehow, was able to get aboard the doomed house and rescue the terrified occupants, Mrs. Mathiesen, her daughter, Vera, and a houseguest, Miss Mary Barclay of North Vancouver.

When news of the disaster reached the Tunnel Camp, rescue parties were swiftly organized and began the descent down the steep winding trail to the battered Beach village. Enroute they passed a fill whose culvert had become choked with mud and debris. The incessant pounding of the creek caused nearly one-third of the fill to be washed away, leaving the railway track which ran along the top suspended in mid-air. Over this perilous bridge crawled some 50 miners from Tunnel Camp. Although it swayed with the weight of one or two men it never gave way.

"This party rushed to the town," said *the Province*, "and immediately began the search. The entire place was in darkness and it was only with the greatest difficulty that work carried on. A long rope was stretched across that part of town where the flood continued to pour down and by this means it was possible for the men to cross from side to side. Had they braved the flood alone they would have been swept into the sea. A wall of water 70 feet in width and from three to five feet in depth rushed through the town."

Dr. Menzies and Nurse M. Thionen, aided by trained first aid men, worked ceaselessly treating the inured who were taken to the hospital, which fortunately escaped the havoc which destroyed the town, although it was cut off from the main section of Britannia Beach by the torrent. On the opposite side of the rampaging river, which had cut a new course through the heart of the community, an improvised hospital and shelter was established in E.J. Donohue's home where nearly 50 persons were billeted.

Next day, said *the Province*, "nature as if relenting of her mad prank has withheld the terrible rain of the past few days from the stricken little village."

"On Friday, Britannia was a show place as industrial communities go, with pretty houses set in neat gardens. Today a tangled mass of trees, boulders and the wreckage of homes cut the village in two."

"Had the moving picture show been running, which usually drew large crowds," *the Province* noted, "it is possible that many lives would have been saved."

"In one house the bathroom equipment has been moved bodily and set up in the centre of the comfortably furnished drawing room. A huge enamel bath with a basin nearby, has been set right down in the centre of the room as if by design of the house owner. Many similar pranks have been played by the headlong rush of water."

The only buildings left undamaged on the residential side were the customs house, moving picture hall, amusement hall and a few Japanese homes. On the mill side, only the store, hotel, office building, some of the mill shop buildings, and the general manager's house remained.

"The place," said Father McDonald, "looks like a prairie town which has been struck by a cyclone."

Assistance from Vancouver was soon forthcoming, although there was no shortage of food and clothing as the store had remained intact. The Vancouver Board of Trade, the Associated Boards of Trade and the Made-in-British Columbia Campaign combined to raise relief money for the victims, and with generous company assistance, all claims were quickly settled.

Britannia Beach, wrecked by the rampaging waters of Britannia Creek. BMM #13729 (top) and 13553 (below)

Shattered homes of Britannia, the result of the Great Flood.
BMM #12892 (top) and 11515 (bottom)

Homes drifted out to sea following the flood. BMM #11523 (top) and 13723 (bottom)

Debris, the aftermath of the disaster. BMM #13645

Furniture piled up on the Store following the disaster. BMM #13024

Not exactly where it should be. Flood damage. BMM #12883

Colonel Perry looks at the havoc in front of the mine office. BMM #12662

She'll have a lot of cleaning up to do. BMM #12645

Bulk loading, SS Quadra, 1923. BMM #12856

SS Quadra, ore carrier to Tacoma, was once a survey ship and ended up as a rumrunner. BMM #13735

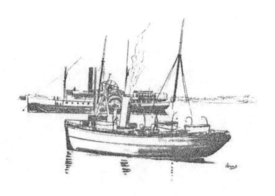

5

SPUN YARN AND GROG

Britannia's "navy" did not rule the waves, but to those who love tales of the sea, the two units which comprised the mining company's "fleet" had more than just a little glamour about them.

Late in 1916 the company began negotiations to acquire the Canadian government survey ship *Quadra* and the hulk of the former Canadian Pacific Steamship Company's *Princess Louise* for the purpose of hauling concentrates down to the smelter at Tacoma. Once upon a time even mention of the names of these ships conjured up in the minds of seafaring people epic tales of spit-and-polish, derring-do and excitement. By 1916 they were past their prime and were far from being things of beauty. Today they are all but forgotten.

For nearly a quarter of a century *Quadra* had with her most famous master, Captain John Walbran, followed the tradition of Captain Richards and HMS *Plumper* in marking on the charts the inlets, the bays, the rocks, the shoals and the channels as a guide to seamen utilizing the jagged British Columbia coast line. When these duties were done she became a lighthouse tender. She was built in 1891 at Paisley, Scotland, and was named in honor of the Spanish officer and gentleman, Don Juan Francisco de la Bodega y Quadra, governor of Nootka in 1792, a man whom Captain Vancouver held in the highest esteem. The career of this trim ship had not been particularly exciting just routine, up to this date, and her days of thrills lay ahead. Just before the negotiations between the government and the Britannia company were completed, *Quadra* was in collision with the CPR steamer *Charmer* in Nanaimo harbor and had to be benched, and so it was, in more or less derelict condition that *Quadra* joined the service of the Britannia Mining and Smelting Company. Never again would her brass be polished, nor would she be the proud ship she once had been.

Far more exciting a story lay behind the old sidewheeler *Princess Louise*, formerly called the *Olympic*. She was built in New York in 1869 at a cost of $200,000 for a shipping man by the name of George White who planned to put her on the run between Victoria and Puget Sound ports. She was the pride of the coast, an amazing vessel for that period. She was 184 feet long, with a 30-foot beam and registered 544 tons. Her hull was made of the finest white oak. Captain James Bolger sailed her around the Horn and on December 7, 1869 she made her first triumphant trip from Olympia, Washington, to Victoria. For two years the *Olympic* was the queen of the northwestern waters, until that day when a rival appeared on the scene in the person of Captain E.A. Starr who placed the *North Pacific* in service as opposition. From the moment the newcomer arrived on the scene the competition of business was fierce. A rate war soon began and fares dropped from $16.50 to 50 cents for a trip between Victoria and Port Townsend. At one stage both steamers tempted passengers and a chromo, a chromo being a lithographed picture which usually depicted such stirring and patriotic scenes as "Wellington at Waterloo". It is said that wars of any kind seldom solve problems, and rate wars in particular fit into that theory. The two new captains, D.B. Finch of the *Olympic* and E.A. Starr of the *North Pacific*, finally agreed to end the feud in one glorious battle royal. Like jousting knights of old, they agreed to hold a race across the Straits of Juan de Fuca, and the winner would take all and the loser would retire from service.

In Victoria there was terrific wagering as to the outcome of the battle, with full support going to the *Olympic* from that quarter. There seemed to be more sympathy for the *North Pacific* on the other side of the border and the Americans heaped their "gold eagles" on her.

On a warm morning in June 1871 the two sidewheelers ploughed through the Straits of Juan de Fuca from Victoria to Port Townsend.

Black smoke belched from their funnels; cheering passengers lined the rails, and when the two contestants pulled in close to one another, there were catcalls from one side to the other. The captains would order more steam, and the "black gangs" tossed the furniture into the fire boxes in compliance. But that evening in Victoria there was no happiness, the *Olympic* had struck out, losing by three minutes.

As a result the *Olympic* went to San Francisco, and the Starr's, as per agreement when the wager was set-up paid her a subsidy to keep away from Puget Sound which sometimes ran as high as $50,000 per annum. She returned to the northwest in 1878 and was purchased from the Hudson's Bay Company and renamed *Princess Louise* in honor of the Duchess of Argyle. In 1883 the Hudson's Bay Company sold her to Captain John Irving's Canadian Pacific Navigation Company and she was placed on the Vancouver-Victoria run. When Irving sold out to the Canadian Pacific Railway Company in 1901, she passed into the hands of this great concern. But the days of the *Princess Louise* were numbered. New and faster steamships appeared and the crown she had once worn so proudly now belonged to others. Finally, old and tired, she was taken to Coal Harbor to die. She was stripped down to the hull and converted to a barge. Her walking beam, erroneously thought many years later to have belonged to the Hudson's Bay Company steamer *Beaver*, was displayed at Prospect Point.

Princess Louise's service with the Britannia Company was not long in years. She was subsequently acquired by the Whalen pulp and paper interests who operated a pulp mill at Woodfibre, opposite Britannia, and in 1919 she came to an inglorious end by sinking wearily at her moorings at Port Alice at the northern tip of Vancouver Island where the Whalens had other pulp and paper interests.

As for the *Quadra*, a new company was formed in 1918 to operate her, known as the Quadra Steamship Company, a wholly-owned subsidiary of the Britannia Mining and Smelting Company. For nearly six years, under the command of Captain C.C. Cutler, *Quadra* carried bulk ore down to Tacoma. In May 1924 she was sold to a Vancouver marine broker, A.R. Bissett who promptly chartered the proud little lady into the booze trade.

Her final year of life was told by George Winterburn, the *Quadra's* second engineer, in the Province magazine section for September 14, 1957.

"In the summer of 1924 she was chartered by a rum-running company which was operating on a large scale. It was then that I joined as second engineer. The full complement consisted of a supercargo, captain, two mates, three engineers and a crew of eight. The supercargo was the commodore of the expedition; he was the supreme boss; even the captain taking orders from him.

"The ship was then altered to make it suitable for long voyages – four to five months in rum-row without touching port was a normal stretch of duty. If the ship's stores ran short, the launches would bring out what was required from shore.

"We loaded up in Vancouver with 22,000 cases of choice liquors, wines, rums and even a large quantity of beer which was all consigned to Ensenada in Mexico. Papers were arranged to show that we had all been there, discharged our cargo and left again with a clear bill of health. This we had before we even left Vancouver. It was a clear, calm moonlight night when we were proceeding down the Straits of Juan de Fuca towards the open sea when the engine room telegraph rang down to "stop". This was a fine night for doing business and we did plenty of it. Several launches came off to meet us and upon presenting their credentials consisting of one-half of a one dollar bill that had to be matched with the other half that the supercargo kept, the order was filled and away he went to shore with his launch full of liquor.

"Before daylight we again got underway and did not stop until we were abreast of Astoria where we conducted more business. It was here that we really sent liquor ashore, which no doubt found its way to the Portland market. It began to look as if our intended four months' voyage was going to be considerably shortened and we had been at sea barely a week.

"We left Astoria for San Francisco where we took up our position just outside the Farallone Islands which are 50 miles offshore from the Golden Gate. It was here that a bad storm hit us, causing us to heave-to for a whole week. It was too stormy for any boats to come off, so we could not do any business nor could we run for shelter from the storm on account of the contraband. All we could do was "sacking" – which means removing the liquor from the cases and sewing it up in sacks of 12 which are not only easier to handle but not quite so obvious to the curious. Finally the storm blew itself out and the weather got warm and balmy. Business got brisk and in no time we were left with only half the cargo.

"Two other ships in the vicinity were operating for the same company and as they had both been in these waters a long time, it was decided that we would take the remainder of their cargoes, which gave us more than we started with. Both of these ships were wooden schooners; one a two-master called the *Coal Harbor*; the other a five-master called the *Malahat*.

"While working alongside the *Malahat*, due to a miscalculation in seamanship, we rammed her instead, but as she was built of stout British Columbia fir, it was quite resilient and suffered no damage except a few scratches. Our own ship suffered badly but remained afloat, as the damage was above the waterline. Our bowspirit was snapped off like a match stick and our graceful clipper bow stove in, leaving a gaping hole into which we stuffed mattresses to keep the seas out, but each time we dipped into a wave, a few tons of water would get past the mattresses and slosh along the 'tween decks, flooding all the cabins.

"All hands had to help load the launches, even the lookout, and had he been on his job maybe this story might never have been written, as this ship was the first big ship to be caught. We had drifted to within two miles of the Farallone Island when a U.S. Coast Guard cutter came up with bow gun trained on us. The gun was a 12-pounder but when a person is looking down the wrong way the gun has the appearance of a 15-incher. He fired a warning shot at a launch which tried to slip away. That proved conclusively to us that he meant business and would not take a few cases of liquor to let us go. We later found that he had received a bribe of $20,000 from our rival company to capture us.

"Our skipper protested the arrest on the grounds that we were more than an hour's steaming time from the U.S. coast, which was at the time the recognized legal position of Rum Row. The protestations did not good. He ordered us to proceed to San Francisco and when our captain refused he put a prize crew aboard and towed us in. But when the prize crew was being transferred back to the cutter on completion of the tow, all hands with the exception of the officer in charge had to be taken aboard in cargo nets. During the tow I secreted seven cases of whisky down the double bottom tank in the engine room, then flooded it so that in case we should lose our cargo but get the ship back we would at least have some fortification against melancholia or seasickness, but alas, we were taken ashore next morning and I have never laid eyes on her since.

"She sank her moorings in the Bay and took with her my seven cases of whisky.

"Thus ends the story of the good ship *Quadra*, but the crew were not signed off for another seven months. We were living in hotels in San Francisco for six months waiting for the case to come up in court, and when it did it lasted for four weeks. The supercargo, captain and two shoreside agents each got two years and $10,000 fine. The two mates each got 13 months and $1,000 fine. The chief engineer was fined $500. All the rest got off "not guilty" and we were given passage back to Vancouver.

"When the trial was over and the captain of the Coast Guard cutter returned to his ship, he captured and brought in another rum-runner which turned out to belong to our rival company. He was then given another $20,000 to perjure the case. He lost his command, did a year in jail for perjury but came out $40,000 richer."

The seizure of the *Quadra* was made on October 24, 1924 and the final rites were held several years later at a United States marshal's public auction sale in San Francisco. *Quadra* was sold for $1625 to be broken up for scrap.

Settling tanks, No. 3 Mill. BMM #11167

Tube mill floor, No. 3 Mill, 1923. BMM #12915

Underground scene. BMM #14069

Drills roar deep in the heart of the Britannia Mine.
BMM #14072

6

THROUGH SPINDRIFT TO SAFE PORT

Edward Joseph Donohue, a native of Racine, Wisconsin, owed his all to J. W. D. Moodie. He was, therefore, a Moodie man through and through and what Mr. Moodie liked Mr. Donohue liked and what Mr. Moodie didn't like Mr. Donohue didn't like.

Their association had begun years before when they were both at the Tintic mine, near Salt Lake City, Utah. Donohue had been a clerk and Moodie was the boss. One day Donohue went to his immediate superior and asked for the afternoon off so he could catch a baseball game and offered to make up the time by coming to work earlier the next morning. That day Moodie happened to arrive in the office earlier than usual and was startled to see Donohue's "devotion" to his job.

"My God," Moodie exclaimed, "you're the only man around here that's doing a day's work for a day's pay." And with that statement, Donohue's rise began. First of all, Moodie fired the office manager and moved the "hard-working" and devoted Donohue into his spot. When Moodie came up to Britannia he sent for Donohue to become secretary-treasurer of Britannia Mining and Smelting Company.

Donohue's main concern seems to have been with the company store, whose manager was Thomas Miller. Probably much of the dissatisfaction over the operation of the store can be laid at Donohue's feet, for he did not give it the close attention it required, in other words, he overlooked that which should have been obvious. Donohue's dealing with the employees has been described as resembling the attitude of the Czar of Russia towards his peasant-subjects: haughty, removed and "Moodieish".

The three-storey building which housed the company store was stocked with enough goods to supply a city the size of New Westminster – everything from suites of furniture down to notions, and the quantity of each item in the inventory was always high. Mr. Donohue liked to order in quantity, particularly from friends, so that the salesman would get a good commission. (From his brother-in-law down in Salt Lake City, for instance, he gave a huge order for sterling silver spoons – far more than were needed.)

When Donohue became general manager, succeeding B.B. Nieding, who stayed only a few days, he would pass out raises to a few, but not to everybody. This caused jealousies and hard feeling, and rather than being on the merit basis, they seemed to be granted on a whim of his. For instance, if one of the men in the store got a raise and mentioned it to others, it was only natural that they too, would appear before the czar to share in largess being bestowed. One moment Donohue would be in a good mood and the next a black cloud would seem to descend and he would bellow at the suppliant servant, "You'll get a raise when I'm damn good and ready to give you one. Get out!"

To the officers of the company at head-office in New York, it was felt that Donohue wasn't cutting the mustard. If the mine were to be kept going in these trying times, it needed a real mining man to run it, and on top of that, the question of the orderly conduct of the store was being questioned. On January 26, 1922 Donohue sent his resignation to the directors. At the February 8 meeting of the board, Carleton Perkins Browning was appointed general manager. Under his management the whole tone of employee-employer relations changed radically, and for the better, and when in 1948, he retired, the employees went out of their way to do him honor.

Browning had joined the company in 1914 after completing his studies at Columbia University where he had met E.B. Schley. His first job at Britannia was as a rodman with the engineering department and he had risen steadily in the company hierarchy.

Now that he was in charge of the operation, Browning gave prime consideration to the store, which was of the utmost importance to the people of Britannia. W.A. Matheson, who had succeeded Donohue as secretary-treasurer in 1921, suggested the store be turned into a co-operative and this met with the immediate approval of W.J. Quigly, vice-president. A record was kept of all purchases made by the employees, either charge or cash, and every six months an audit was taken and a dividend declared. The first of these bonuses was declared on January 30, 1924 – a dividend of 14 per cent.

Meanwhile, on February 15, 1923, a year after Donohue left Britannia, W.J. Quigly filed charges against the former general manager. It was alleged $80,000 had been misappropriated, and, as *The Vancouver Sun* noted, there was a nation-wide search out for Donohue. On March 15 he gave himself up to police in Oklahoma City and voluntarily came back to Vancouver to face the charges. On October 24, 1923, he went on trial before Mr. Justice Gregory, and as the evidence began to unfold it was apparent the Crown had no case. The jury was out for only a few minutes before returning a "not guilty" verdict, after the judge told them he would, without hesitation, have taken the case from the jury had not the defence wanted a clear vindication.

On the mining side of the events for the year, the Victoria Mine was proving to be exceedingly rich and the bachelor camp up there was expanding rapidly.

A new process of extracting ore was introduced in 1924 called "leaching" or the "precipitation" process from a plant at the 1000-foot level on Jane Flats. Simply put, the process worked like this: if you take a spoonful of sugar and dump it into a glass it will disappear from sight and yet the taste of the sugar remains. In the same way, very hard rocks can dissolve in water, although more slowly, of course, than sugar. Some of the rock in the mine slowly dissolves and puts copper in the mine-water that flows down Britannia Creek and into Howe Sound. The leaching process removes this valuable mineral content so it will not be wasted. The mine water is channelled into a series of troughs into which has been placed pieces of scrap iron and "tin" cans. The copper comes out of the water and the iron dissolves. The residue of this natural mining process is scooped up and sent to the smelter for processing.

The operation proved immensely successful and the Jane Flat plant, along with several smaller ones, was in operation until 1928 when a much larger one was built at the Townsite. A second plant was put in at the Beach in 1955.

Where do the cans come from? Strange as it may seem in this age of waste, they are not as easy to come-by as might be expected. Today (1966) they are brought in by the trunkload from Victoria on Vancouver Island. Production figures were rising rapidly and in 1926, for the first time in the history of the mine, more than a million tons of ore were milled. New buildings were being erected for the welfare of the employees at both the Townsite and the Beach. At both places, gymnasiums, 40 x 160 feet, were built in 1925, and on the flat at the Beach between the general offices and the recreation hall, swings and sea-saws were erected for the children. The following year a one-storey staff house was built at the Townsite and at the Victoria camp a bank of three bowling alleys was added to the side of No. 1 bunkhouse.

The Britannia mine was now gaining world attention for the economical way the copper was being extracted, and in 1927 the provincial mineralogist stated in his report to the minister of mines "even the proverbial 'squeal' is saved in the concentrator," although, alas, he gives us no indication as to what use the noise was put to.

The important work for 1927 was the completion of a haulage tunnel on the 2700 foot level which was driven both from the surface and from the bottom of the No. 3 shaft. This tunnel was extended through to the Fairview, giving it a total length of 11,220 feet, though which the total output of the mine was taken and dumped into the raise, and from there it was hauled to the concentrator.

Browning's accomplishments were something to boast about, and the mineralogist was impressed with the "well planned efficiency in every department." So, too, was Canada's governor general, Lord Willingdon, who arrived at the Beach on April 12, 1927 for an official visit.

"His Excellency," reported the *Vancouver Morning Star*, "was welcomed at the wharf by the entire population of the village, school children being drawn up in order with flags. The children sang "O Canada" and "God Save the King", and Lord Willingdon, after addressing them briefly, requested they be given a holiday for the rest of the day."

"After luncheon at the residence of A.C. Munroe, the mine manager, the governor-general and his party were dressed up in overalls, gumboots and miner's caps with acetylene lamps attached, for a trip through the mine." They were taken up the cable line said the Star, "and travelled for several miles by railway underground."

Willingdon lingered in Britannia longer than his schedule called for and was late for dinner at the Vancouver Club.

Britannia was now reaching its prime, and in 1928 a record production was set. That year 1,661,325 tons of ore, an increase of more than a quarter million tons over the previous year, was handled by the mill. Nearly 1100 men were on the payroll as the giddy and gay 1920s headed uncontrolled towards disaster. At the Townsite a wooden sidewalk from the store right through town had been built. "This," said the company report for 1927 "keeping the children off the track and providing a safe walk much needed in the camp." A two room school house was built at the Beach and a room added to the mine school. At Victoria, the top of the old ore bin was filled in to make room for a small gymnasium, and at the townsite, a two storey house was converted into a church, with the Roman Catholics using one floor and the Protestants the other.

In 1928 A.C. Munroe put his "pride and joy" into operation. It was an electric furnace foundry, built to his design, which produced the major amount of castings for the property as well as all the grinding balls used in the concentrator. The foundry was so successful that plants of similar design were built in Flin Flon, Manitoba, Spokane, Washington, and in Africa.

Early in 1929, still riding the crest of the boom, the company organized a subsidiary, the Torbit Mining Company Ltd. to develop the Toric group of claims near Alice Arm in the Portland Canal area of northern British Columbia. Before development work and the construction of a road into the property could be completed, the bottom fell out of the stock market in the United States, and the whole of North America, from that grim October day, began to enter that bitter period known as the Great Depression.

The last year of the boom had been a good one for Britannia. E.B. Schley had told the stockholders "we believe the Company's shareholders will be satisfied," but the following year the picture was far from being satisfactory.

"The outlook for copper," noted the Report at the Minister of Mines for British Columbia, "is anything but encouraging." The price of copper dropped to the record low of 5 ⅞ cents per pound. The output of Britannia fell off by nearly 200,000 tons and the concentrator was operating on a part-time basis only.

Schley told the stockholders in 1931 of a "general reduction of salaries of all officers and employees...made effective during the year and your Directors commend the unselfish efforts of the entire organization in their endeavor to obtain the best possible operating results during a year of many discouragements."

The efforts of C.P. Browning to keep going were recognized by the Canadian Institute of Mining and Metallurgy in 1931 by the awarding of the Randolph Bruce gold medal, awarded for the most distinguished service to the mining industry in Canada.

The committee's recommendation of Mr. Browning was based on the following accomplishments, which were recorded in the *1931 Report of the B.C. Minister of Mines.*

"(1) Successfully mining, even under the present extremely difficult copper-market conditions, an ore of approximately one per cent copper content. To accomplish this Mr. Browning has, through his organizing genius, maintained his costs for the year 1931 at a little under 75 cents per ton for all mining and milling operations. This is not only important in itself, but it should give tremendous encouragement to the development of low-grade ore-bodies in Canada. While it is difficult to say how much of the credit for any mining accomplishment is due to the ability and efforts of the general manager, those who are closely in touch with the credit should be given to Mr. Browning for his remarkable organizing ability, his inspiring leadership and his technical skill.

"(2) During the present severe depression and in spite of the necessity for reducing costs to a minimum, Mr. Browning has so managed the work that the community of Britannia Beach has been supported so effectually that there has been no reduction in the number of families in the community.

"(3) Mr. Browning has always been an active and consistent supporter of our Institute, of its British Columbia Division, of community life at Britannia, and of all things tending to promote the welfare of our industry and of our country."

Despite Browning's efforts to keep the camp going, the layoffs began in 1932. The staff was reduced from the high of 1100 men in 1928 to 548, and added to the troubles of the mine was a four cents a pound tariff placed by the United States government on copper brought into the country. Another difficulty also arose at the same time. "The position taken by the British government," said the mining report, "in disallowing the four cents per pound preference for Canadian copper not treated in Canada has placed Britannia in a very serious position and may result in the closing down of the property – a disaster under present circumstances."

As a result, the Howe Sound Company's report for 1932 stated "the copper thereafter produced at Britannia, when sold, must be marketed abroad and arrangements for such disposal of the product have been perfected on a basis which, it is believed, will be as satisfactory in operation as has that governing the sales of lead and zinc produced in Mexico."

Thus it was that Britannia was not the happy camp it had been when Lord Willingdon had visited it in 1927. On September 8, 1932, the camp had its second vice-regal visit, this time by Lord Bessborough. Although he went underground, made the usual speeches and carried on his expected duties, His Lordship felt "indisposed" that day and did not enter into the spontaneous enthusiasms which his predecessor had done. In 1933 the price of gold was raised and the golden bloom flowered on the B.C. economy. The Bridge River camps, the Pioneer and Bralorne, were in full production, and up in the Cariboo, the old town of Barkerville, scene of one of the greatest gold rushes in the history of mining in the 1860s, was coming back to life. There, on Cow Mountain, overlooking Jack of Clubs Lake and the famed Lowhee placer property, the gamble of veteran prospector Fred Wells and Dr. W.B. Burnett and O.F. Sollibake, was paying off and the Cariboo Gold Quartz Mine was a reality and not a stock promotion as many, including leading geologists, had warned.

Britannia Mining & Smelting Company joined in the new Cariboo rush by taking under option the Black Jack and Westport groups, owned by two Barkerville oldtimers, Fred J. Tregillus and Tommy Blair, plus the Wintrip property on Stouts Gulch. Subsequently the Britannia company became interested in the Midas claims between French Snowshoe and Little Snowshoe Creeks, 13 miles by pack train from Keithley Creek. All these options, though, were subsequently allowed to lapse.

Gradually the mining picture in British Columbia began to improve. The mine, instead of operating on a 10 per cent basis, was by 1934 on a 20 per cent basis, and for the first time, high grade zinc concentrates, assaying 54 per cent were shipped from Britannia to the smelter.

"These shipments," noted the mining report, "could not be made under normal production conditions as the general run of the mine ore would not contain enough zinc to make the separation worthwhile." In other words, Browning went after the zinc to keep the men working.

By 1937 the worst was over. The price of copper rose and E.B. Schley was able to tell Howe Sound Company shareholders that the Britannia property "was operated continuously at normal tonnage capacity and contributed materially to consolidated earnings."

On the international scene, one Adolf Hitler was on centre stage. He had already gobbled up Austria and was eyeing Czechoslovakia and Poland. Italy had nabbed Ethiopia, and Japan was in the field against China.

Where, and when, would the next blow fall?

Bandstand at the Townsite, 1930. BMM #13208

Pillow fight during water sports events at the Townsite pool, July 1, 1937. BMM #13206

Snow along the track near the Tunnel Townsite, 1938. BMM #13056

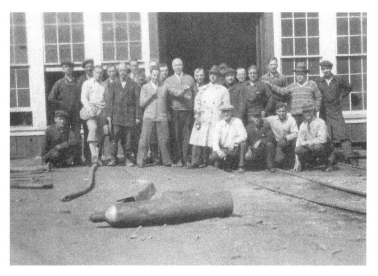

Visit of Jimmy McLarnin to the Townsite. Front row, left to right: Geoff Emery, Sam McLarnin, C. Henderson, Jimmy McLarnin, Bob Dick, C.V. Brennan, C. Dobson. Kneeling: W. Warranson, Dave MacDonald, A. Stork, A. Dove. Identified in the back row is A. Stewart. BMM #13417

Rock drilling contest at the Townsite, July 1, 1930. BMM #13209

Empress Camp, 1936. BMM #12875

Victoria Hotel, with framing shed in the foreground. BMM #13466

Surface plant, Victoria Camp, 1929, showing No. 1 shaft, compressor house, ore bin, dry kiln, Beta tram terminal and the 1800 portal. BMM #13460

7

MINE-MILL ONE OF THE FAMILY

Despite the "peace in our time" promise made after Munich by the Right Honorable Neville Chamberlain, prime minister of Great Britain, the war drums continued to beat ominously in Europe.

At Britannia, in these last days of peace, in the bunkhouses at both the Beach and the Townsite, the men were talking quietly about forming a union. It was not the first time such a subject had been on the minds of Britannia miners. As early as 1913, the Industrial Workers of the World, better known as the Wobblies, had tried to organize, and pickets had been set up at the Terminal Navigation Dock in Vancouver. Men marched back and forth with placards bearing the wording, "Don't be a scab, don't go to Britannia." The organizers of this attempt at organization, however, soon were on the receiving end of J.W.D. Moodie's celebrated order to pack up and get out. Three years later, in 1917, two brothers, Roy and Jack McKenzie, attempted to organize the Western Federation of Miners at the Townsite, but it was a pretty hopeless task. In the first place, the brothers knew very little about how to go about organizing a union, and secondly, and what was probably more important, management's attitude towards unions had not changed since the Wobblies' attempt. Meetings were held at the Townsite and quite a few of the miners signed up. The principal demand was for better wages which at the time were $3.00 a day for miners and $2.75 for muckers. Recklessly, as it turned out, they put their demands to management, and to back it up, staged a one-day strike, which was put down simply by ordering the ring-leaders to get out of town.

A small strike occurred about 1931 in the Foundry down at the Beach, when the Japanese walked away from their jobs demanding better pay and improved working conditions. The men weren't fired, but they didn't get any more money either, although their working conditions were slightly improved afterwards. The Japanese had hoped for white support in their demands, but it didn't work out that way.

Further attempts at union organization were frustrated because visitors to the camp had to obtain a pass before entering company property, and company property was everywhere. However, in 1939 some of the men decided to make another stab at organizing, and as before, the talk and the signing-up of members had to be done in secret. This time wages were not the main issue, for these were depression times, and the men felt themselves lucky to be even drawing a cheque. The concern was for safety and health conditions. Another factor which brought the men together was the food served in the bunkhouses and they demanded the elimination of double decker bunks. The last point was particularly vexing, for despite government regulations forbidding the men to bring their own blankets into a mining camp, bedbugs flourished, particularly in the double deckers. However, before the necessary percentages of men could be signed up, the secret leaked out, and late one night in April 1939, the five ring leaders were called from their beds to report to the mine office where they were told their services at Britannia were no longer required and to get the next boat down to Vancouver. The rank-and-file who had signed up weren't exactly fired for their association with the trade unionists, but they were marked men. For instance, at the end of May, many went down to Vancouver to see King George VI and Queen Elizabeth, and some overstayed their leave. If they have been associated with the attempt to organize a union they were fired, otherwise those who were AWOL just got their knuckles rapped.

Britannia had never been noted for its safety record. Accidents in the mines and in the machine shops had been prevalent for years, largely due, it is said, because of the inexperience of the miners and the steady turnover of the working force. A small beginning was made in 1923 when St. John Ambulance first aid courses were given, to be followed, six years later, by the establishing of a branch of the Association at Britannia. The inaugural meeting was held in the Movie Hall at the Townsite on February 11, 1929, and it is interesting to note, that the Minute Book which was to be used right up to 1953 had originally served as a record book for the Rossland branch from 1915 to 1916. The company encouraged these early classes, by establishing, in 1926, the Britannia Mining and Smelting Company trophy, and the competitions for this cup became one of the major annual events at the mine. At one time there were 12 senior, four junior and two ladies' teams competing. Two years later, in 1928, the company set aside some money for a "safety sweepstake". The sum amounted to $300 per shift, and a deduction was made from this amount every time an accident occurred. A draw was held quarterly for the balance, and over the years, with modifications from time to time, it became a useful tool to stress safety, although it still did not cut down the accident statistics as much as had been hoped. For instance, in 1923, there were 248 compensation cases at Britannia.

Safety officials at the mine also tried a bonus system to cut down the accident rate by focussing their attention on the shift boss. For the first accident free month the shift boss got a $10.00 bonus, for the second, $12.50 and for the third and every accident free month after that, $15.00. Like the other scheme, it was not the real answer to the vexing problem of mine safety, and what that answer was was as elusive as the Scarlet Pimpernel. But this was not fiction, and the statistics of accidents, fatal and non-fatal, make grim reading.

In September 1939 the German army invaded Poland, and Canada, along with Britain and France declared war on the Third Reich. Recruiting officers appeared at both the Beach and the Townsite and many joined the three armed services. Manpower became increasingly short and unskilled workers stepped in to take the place of those who had enlisted to add to the seemingly unending problem of safety. Several programs were drawn up to try to educate the men that it was to their advantage to acquaint themselves with safety routines and courses, such as "Job Instruction Training", "Job Safety Training," "Job Relations Training" and "Job Method Training" were drawn up, and although the courses were not compulsory, the men were urged to take them, just as they were the St. John Ambulance first aid courses.

The employment situation grew particularly acute when the shipyards of the Lower Mainland began to lure away the miners and workmen by offering high wages, plus overtime. Eventually this drain-off was stopped by the federal government putting a manpower freeze on the mining industry, and those working in this endeavour couldn't leave their jobs.

The war created a demand for copper, but the war had taken away the manpower with which to operate the mine efficiently. Thus the mine could not be put into full production and there was nobody to undertake that work most vital to the life of the mine – development. And so there began that period of the mine's history in which it was, literally, "worked on its own fat", using up those reserves which had been previously blocked out, and not developing new ore bodies. In 1943 the ore problem became serious, and the following year, the mine was in a precarious position.

Meanwhile, the war had been going badly for the Allies. France had fallen, the Soviet Union was being attacked, and in December 1941, the war spread to the Pacific Region following the sneak attack by the Japanese on Pearl Harbor, Hawaii. That night, December 7, as the people of Britannia huddled around their radio sets listening to the grim details of that "day of infamy" as President Roosevelt called it, some of the men recalled a rather strange conversation which had taken place a few months previously with one of the Japanese workmen.. This man had called at one of the bunkhouses with a load of washing and asked the men to settle up their accounts with him immediately, as "we'll be leaving soon, but when we come back, we'll be the bosses." The remark had, at the time, seemed rather silly, and it was treated as a joke. There were other stories, too, and considering the panic of the time, they were inevitable. There were reports of high frequency radio transmitters on the property or back in the woods. Such stories were a dime a dozen up and down the coast, and while these incidents, true or untrue, were being talked about, one point, strongly in favor of the Japanese in British Columbia, was largely overlooked: many had sons – and daughters – in the Canadian armed forces. Also, the majority of the Japanese were just as stunned and angry at the turn of events as were their white fellow workers. Nobody can be proud of the treatment meted out to those of Japanese origin living on the West Coast. They were all branded as security risks, and in a shocking manner, were uprooted from their homes and shipped off to camps in the interior of the province. The last of the

Japanese left Britannia on May 8, 1942, never to come back. As the Japanese moved away, one family after another, their homes were taken over by the white workers. There were few expressions of regret, or of sympathy, but there was one which deserved at least a bit of recognition. A group of school boys down at the Beach pooled their savings to buy a watch for one of their schoolmates who, because of his racial background, was forced to move. It was not possible under the circumstances to make a formal presentation, but it was made outside the school building. There were no speeches, both the donors and the recipients were embarrassed, but in the manner of young boys, the thought was there and they had expressed it in the only way they could.

The attack on Pearl Harbor had brought the war to the threshold of western North America. The question was now: When, if, and where would the forces of the Mikado strike next? Maybe British Columbia itself would be the next target. There were rumors that an invasion force had been sighted, but had turned back when an R.C.A.F. patrol plan had spotted the fleet and turned in the alarm. There were other rumors of a Japanese aircraft carrier operating off the coast, and there were fears that enemy bombs would soon be falling. That B.C. might experience an enemy air attack was considered by the authorities to be a strong possibility, and one of the first steps taken was to organize volunteer corps known as the A.R.P. (Air Raid Precautions). One such group was formed at Britannia. Another precaution taken was the forming of the Pacific Coast Militia Rangers which was set-up along military lines, but was conspicuous by its lack of spit and polish. If the Japanese had invaded the West Coast, these Rangers would have provided the back-bone of our defences. Uniforms and rifles were issued to them and the men were given a quick, but basic course in how to deal with the invaders. At Britannia, a rifle range was established at the gravel pit, and targets, attached to a wire, were set up to provide moving objects to shoot at. The first shot fired missed the target but snapped the wire, and thus the Britannia platoons had to stick to stationery targets. Route marches were organized, aircraft identification was taught, as was signalling and the watchword was security. Suppose, said the instructor, there was "Quisling" at Britannia. (Twenty-five years ago the name "Quisling" was synonymous with "traitor", having its origin in Vidkum Quisling who betrayed Norway to the Germans at the time of the Nazi invasion.) The answer to the instructor's question was simply that "It can't happen here, we know everybody in camp." But one night a man went into the power house and sat idly chatting with the operator, and while enjoying a cup of coffee, pulled a gun out of his pocket and told the astonished operator that the power house was now in "enemy" hands. Of course, the "Quisling" was only acting the role, but it pointed out forcibly that such an act could happen at Britannia, even though everybody knew everybody else.

Equally important to the defence of British Columbia was the A.R.P., which would swing into action in the event of air attack. The volunteer members were taught first aid, fire fighting, etc., and in co-operation with the local Red Cross Corps they were prepared to meet any emergency. They were particularly careful to see that all homes were equipped with black out curtains, and when the first black out of the entire province was ordered they felt secure in the knowledge that they had done their work well. However, a naval patrol vessel soon dispelled that. In their zeal they had forgotten to black out the concentrator, and the blazing lights of this plant shone out like a beacon. It was an embarrassment which was quickly corrected.

The ladies, too, went to war. With Mrs. C.P. Browning as commandant, two sections of the Red Cross were organized at Britannia. The one consisting of the younger ladies of the community was classed as the "active" corps, while the senior group was known as the "reserve". The dividing age line was 40, which caused a great deal of anxiety to border line cases. But "war is hell" anyway and the ladies sometimes were not quite accurate in putting their ages on the form. Thus there were a lot of 39 year olds, but hardly any 40 year olds. Like the men in the Militia, they went swinging along on route marches, learned how to make bed pans out of newspapers, gave out ration books, and learned how to live off the land. This particular course nearly led to revolution at Britannia, but luckily for the ladies their zeal was controlled before it was too late. Their course had indicated that a tasty salad could be made from skunk cabbage leaves and they planned to serve it to their menfolk for dinner one night. Saner heads prevailed and "the pax Britannia" continued uninterrupted.

An air raid shelter was set up in one of the old mine tunnels, and during air raid drills the ladies would lead the children out of the two communities to safety, where, once inside the shelter, they would be taken care of by the reservists. They also made bandages for overseas hospitals, knit socks, sent parcels to their fighting men, took over the cleaning of the company offices, and that holy of holies, that all-male sanctuary, the club house.

Thus, along with purchasing Victory Bonds and War Savings Certificates, and contributing to patriotic funds, did Britannia join with the rest of the nation in its war efforts.

While all effort was made to combat the enemy, should he arrive, an enemy, at least in the eyes of the management, did arrive, and when the boss was away, he took possession of the camp. His name was Harvey Murphy, organizer for the mine, Mill and Smelter Workers Union. The "invasion" occurred one Saturday in April 1943 and before any counter measures could be taken Britannia was captured. Secretly, Murphy organized a quick meeting at the Beach, passed out membership cards and headed for the Townsite to carry on similar activity, but to his chagrin, found the skip wasn't working that day, so he had to walk up the winding, steep trail. By Monday morning, upon management's return to Britannia, unionism was a fait accompli.

Murphy told Mr. Browning the necessary 51 per cent of employees had signed up, and in reply, Murphy was told by Browning that he didn't feel there was a need for a union, "but if the employees wanted one he felt the union should become one of the family of Britannia." And, even though a charter had not yet been granted, he said he would recognize the union as a bargaining agent for the men right away.

That night, in the Townsite theatre the first "open" union meeting at Britannia was held. In bringing the meeting to order, Harvey Murphy stepped back into history, back to the days of 1917 when the Western Federation of Miners tried to organize in Britannia.

"The meeting which was adjourned in 1917," he said, "will now reconvene."

Temporary officers were elected that night, with Alex Spaden being named president pro-tem. A pledge was given to the men overseas that there would be no disruption on the homefront and there would be no strikes as long as the war continued.

When permanent officers were elected, Jack Balderson was named president and Ken Smith, vice-president. In 1960, Smith, who had started at Britannia in 1936, became national president of the International Union of Mine, Mill and Smelter Workers (Canada).

The year following the initial organization of the union, a charter was issued, and Local 663 came into formal existence as a "member of the Britannia family." A Women's Auxiliary to the union was formed and these two newcomers contributed greatly to the life of both the communities at the Beach as well as the Townsite.

A combined labor-management committee soon got down to business on the old, but still pressing question of mine safety. In 1946 an educational program was set up, which proved so effective that in 1958 a goal which had, in the past been only a dream, was realized. The National Safety Council presented the mine with the award of honor for the greatest safety improvement of any mine in Canada.

Victoria Sawmill, 1926. BMM #13396

Victoria framing machine, 1930. BMM #13465

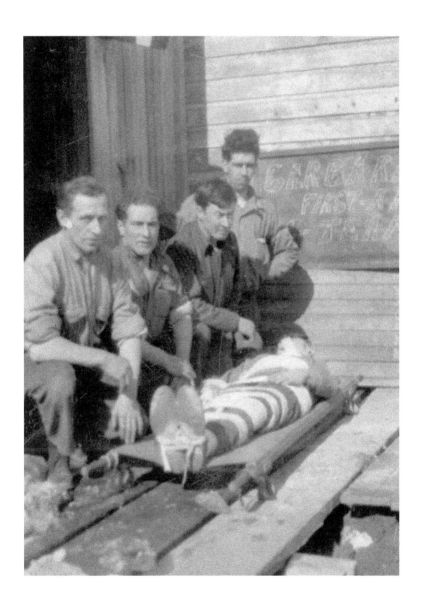

Barbara Camp first aid team, 1930. BMM #14164

The regular 2 pm passenger trip up the Incline, 1941.
BMM #12860

Going on shift at the 2200 level during the 1940's.
BMM #14021

8

ANACONDA COMES OVER THE RIM-ROCK

At long last the war was over. In May, 1945 Germany surrendered, and in August Japan admitted she had been licked and a document of surrender was signed aboard the American battleship USS Missouri.

Those who had left the mine to join up in 1939 and throughout the war years now returned to their jobs. But there were some "whose names live forever more" who did not return.

Their memory is kept alive in a role of honor in the Britannia Community Church. Of the 150 men who signed up from the copper town, nine were killed in action. Their names were J.A. Dalton, T. Galbraith, R. Brace, J. Labelle, N. McKenzie, G.C. McClelland, W. Poulton, N. Sarles and Roy Ferguson.

During 1945 and 1946, Britannia was, in the words of E.C. Roper, "living from hand to mouth". The head office of the Howe Sound Company in New York had laid it severely on the line: If the mine didn't pay it would be closed down. A quota system had been evolved which had to be met, otherwise all would have been "kaput".

Faced with the bleak situation, the people of Britannia pulled up their sleeves and from muckers to the top brass, what was, in fact "a salvage operation" began to hum. The do it or else quota set by New

York was regularly met and even surpassed, and the money received from this surplus was put back into the mine in the form of development work. Attention was focused at first on the tailings dump and its zinc content, for management felt that once again, as there had been in the late 30s, a market would be found for zinc, which at this time was selling at eight or nine cents a pound. It was noted that No. 8 orebody and ore at the 1250 showed good quantities of zinc, and the gamble was taken to stockpile this ore, just in case there should be a demand for it.

A general strike in the B.C. mining industry, which began July 3, 1946, might well have been the death blow for Britannia. Some 2500 miners in B.C. gold and copper camps, including about 300 at Britannia, were seeking a 29 cent an hour wage boost, the 40 hour week and union security. For 114 days the strike dragged on, until Chief Justice Gordon Sloan worked out a formula for settlement which was announced on October 23. Under it the men received a raise of 64 cents a shift for tradesmen and 48 cents a shift for other workers, plus concessions on overtime and shift differentials. His Lordship said these raises were equivalent to 14 cents and 12 cents an hour respectively.

In 1948 the long "reign" of C.P. Browning came to an end, and in his place stepped Edward Cecil Roper, who began work underground at Britannia in 1936. A magnificent farewell party was held in the gym, now the store, and everybody from the two communities turned out. It was an evening for laughs and for tears, and they came to Mr. Browning's eyes easily that night. For months the employees had been digging into old trunks, photograph albums, writing to ex-employees, to gather pictorial material for a presentation album for the Brownings' which would vividly tell the story of their life and times at Britannia. It was all nicely bound in leather, and when the time came for the presentation, Mr. Browning was almost struck dumb with emotion.

As it was in the 1930s, so it was in the late 1940s, Britannia showed a remarkable tenacity for holding on, even though it was touch-and-go. For four cost-cutting, budget-watching, almost miraculous years, Britannia kept busy waiting for zinc to come into its own. And suddenly the faith and hard work paid off. On June 25, 1950, Communist forces from North Korea invaded South Korea and the price of zinc on the London market leaped to 20 cents a pound.

Britannia was ready for the unprecedented demand for this vital base metal, and great was the joy in the offices of the Howe Sound Company. Nothing was too good for Britannia now, and it had been many a long year since a coat of paint had been applied to company buildings, which, of course, meant all the buildings at the Beach and the Townsite.

During those boom years there was only one note of sadness. In 1952 E.B. Schley, who was chairman of the board of the Howe Sound Company, and had visited Britannia on many occasions, died in New York. He was succeeded by his son, Reeve Schley, Jr. Unlike the aftermath of the two world wars, the end of the Korean War in 1953 did not mean an immediate collapse of the price of either zinc or copper, but rough sailing lay ahead.

A few days before Christmas, 1954, the camp was startled by the strange disappearance of the assistant postmaster down at the Beach. His name was John Keith Black, but it was not so much the fact that he had run off which caused the indignation, rather, it was that he had taken with him a money package consigned to the Royal Bank of Canada at Britannia which contained $44,500 pre-Christmas payroll. Black was last seen a few blocks from his bungalow where he lived with his wife and six-month old son, and the Howe Sound area was not to see him again until February 25, 1956 when the dapper 42 year old clerk appeared in police court in Squamish following his arrest at Redickville, Ontario, 65 miles north west of Toronto. It was then learned his real name was John Keith MacDonald, also known as John Clealand Wallace Black, and when he was arrested, he had remarried under the name of John Larson. Mrs. Larson described her husband as a "Bible-quoting, God-fearing husband," but to the Royal Canadian Mounted Police he was one of Canada's most wanted fugitives. Police recovered $25,184 of the loot, and Black, or whatever his name was, got four years for the robbery and an additional two years for bigamy.

In the fall of 1956 the price or copper fell drastically, and at the same time, the company was heavily involved in a cobalt mine at Salmon, Idaho, which was sapping away the financial resources of the Howe Sound Company. In addition, a new smelting plant was opening at Salt Lake City, Utah. The cobalt venture had been the product of the Korean crisis when the U.S. government offered a premium price of $2.25 a pound. The Salmon property was difficult to operate due to metallurgical problems, and hence the cost was reflected in the Britannia situation.

In addition to the Salmon property and the new smelter, the Howe Sound Company was involved with Sherrit-Gordin in a nickel property at Fort Saskatchewan, Manitoba and this further compounded the economy of Britannia. Towards the end of 1957 it seemed that all that was needed was the burial service to end the Britannia story. The company announced it was throwing in the towel as far as Britannia was concerned, but just before Christmas, the mine got a parole. In an unprecedented move, supported by labor, management, the provincial and federal governments, as well as all political parties, Britannia was kept in operation, although on a reduced scale, during the high winter unemployment period. Under the agreement, the company was to assume a continuing loss on the operation, while the union agreed to forego pay increases due them from the previous August and to work weekends at straight pay to keep production costs down to a minimum. The federal government put up a subsidy of $16,000 a month for six months and British Columbia added another $4,000 for a similar period. But even with this support, Britannia was uneasy, and on February 28, 1958 the message everybody had dreaded to receive, arrived at the mine office. The telegram from New York read: "Close down the Britannia operation March 1, continuing decline in the copper market has made it impractical to prolong the operation even with the assistance which has been received."

The news was received with bitterness. The people of Britannia thought they had been betrayed. Newspaper reporters from Vancouver said, truthfully, "Britannia is a sad town". And they quoted one resident who stated, "This Company has taken millions out of Britannia. When it was riding high, it used to tell our union, "We can't give you big wage increases because we've got to put money aside for a rainy day." Well, now the rainy day is here; but where's the money? The way I figure it, if a foreign company decides to close down a mine, the government ought to take it over, kick them out, and run the mine itself." One ironic aspect of the grim situation was that during the height of the crisis, television was piped in for the first time. In the false security of the previous months, many had purchased TV sets, and with the closure of the mine, many had TV but no jobs. "Oh, well," said one of them, "at least we can watch TV."

Gradually the Townsite, or Mount Sheer, became deserted, although those with youngsters in the school waited, impatiently for the end of the school term before pulling up stakes and leaving. By summer, a new ghost town had been born.

The end was in sight too, for the Howe Sound Company. On March 20, 1958 it was announced that an agreement to merge with Haile Mines had been reached and that a new Howe Sound Company, chartered under the laws of the state of Delaware, was to be formed. The new president was a Haile man, William M. Weaver Jr., although Reeve Schley, Jr still remained a board member. There were some, including executive vice president E.C. Roper, who were not in favor of the merger. Until this time the Howe Sound Company had been entirely a mining corporation, but now, following the merger, it would become a manufacturing concern as well. Because he felt that, as a mining man, he could not play the role his office now demanded, Roper resigned, as did several other directors of the old Howe Sound Company.

With the merger, it was also apparent that the days of the old Britannia Mining and Smelting Company were also over. On August 8, 1958, far removed from the mine, an extraordinary general meeting of shareholders was held in New York which passed a special resolution:

"Resolved that the Company be forthwith wound up voluntarily in accordance with the laws of the Province of British Columbia."

John Earle Nelson was appointed liquidator and on December 8, 1958 the assets of the old company passed directly into the hands of the Howe Sound Company. The end came, tersely, on June 12, 1964 when Nelson reported to the Registrar of Companies in Victoria that "The affairs of the Company have been fully wound up." There was no reflection on the past glories of the Britannia Mining and Smelting Company, no remembrance of the struggle for survival, and no recognition to the thousands of men who had toiled in the mines, who had given their lives, or their limbs, to the copper industry. The end was cold, legal and final.

Meanwhile, Britannia was a pretty dismal place from that Leap year day and through the summer of 1958, when other areas of the province were celebrating the centennial of British Columbia. For Donald McGregor, it was particularly bad. Two weeks before the mine was closed down he had purchased the Townsite and the Beach stores and financial disaster now stared him in the face. Others, whose whole lives had been spent at Britannia, faced the prospect of moving into a new and strange environment, a world which was vastly different from the company town in the shadows of the Britannia Range. But jobs were more important than sentiment, and they did, however reluctantly, move away. Only a few stayed on, clinging to the hope that if the mine didn't re-open at least the Beach would survive as a summer resort or residential district.

After nine months Britannia "beat the ghost" and the Howe Sound Company, who were now directly operating the mine without benefit of a subsidiary company, announced on January 3, 1959 that the mine would re-open and A.G. Kirkland of Salt Lake City, became manager. He held this post until May 1960 when D.W. Pringle was named general superintendent.

The Townsite, however, was dead and would never be resurrected. The buildings were either torn down, or were crushed by the weight of the unshoveled snow. It was a sad thing to see the Townsite die the way it did, but copper prices and company politics are notably unromantic.

On January 15, 1963 the Anaconda Copper Company paid several million cash for the property and a new general manager, B.B. Greenlee, arrived to take charge. On August 11, 1964 another strike occurred. For seven months Britannia lay strike bound. Not until March 3, 1965 did life return to "normal" when the strike was settled and the men returned to their jobs.

The Howe Sound Company, although it had been changed drastically and stripped of what had been its crown jewel, lasted until November 24, 1965, when shareholders ratified a change of name. Henceforth it would be known as Howmet Corporation. A grand old name disappeared, the old order had changed, but the mine, located by Dr. A.A. Forbes, continued under the control of one of the largest copper corporations in the world. Its future, just as was its past, measured in the unpredictable world of the copper price market.

Townsite Hospital, July 1944. BMM #11485

Copper precipitation plant, Townsite, 1940. BMM #13835

Winter scene at the Townsite, 1955, showing clubhouse and store. BMM #13359

Snow, deep and crisp, at the Townsite, 1947. BMM #13351

The Union Dock at Britannia Beach, 1948. BMM #2100

Britannia Beach from the Mill trestle, 1947. BMM #2107

Flag raising ceremony, July 1, 1942 sports day at the Townsite.
BMM #13213

Geordie Mitchell running the cracker contest at the Townsite sports day event. BMM #13348

Tree planting ceremony, Easter 1956. G.C. Lipsey, R. Hudson, R. Richards, B. Hurley, R. Galowan, D. Emery, J. Balderson, N. Atkins, G. Hurley. BMM #13403

Britannia Beach pool, 1946. BMM #14115

Wesley D. Black, Townsite school teacher and later BC Government Cabinet Minister at July 1, 1944 celebration. BMM #13306

Tunnel Hotel dining room, winter of 1950. BMM #13249

Britannia Creek trestle at the Townsite which filled a gap made by the flood waters of 1921. BMM #13246

9

TRAILS AFLOAT AND ASHORE

For fifty years the communities which went under the general name of "Britannia", the Beach, the Townsite or Mount Sheer, Victoria, Empress, Jane, etc. were isolated from the bustling world of bright lights which, by looking at a map, seemed to be on their very doorstep. This isolation was Britannia's strength and its greatest inconvenience. Its strength came from the strong community spirit which developed in the camp, which, not surprisingly, came to a sudden end when the road was built along Howe Sound to Vancouver, and with it, the southern extension of the Pacific Great Eastern Railway from Squamish to North Vancouver. Until this highway was built in 1957 the only way to get in or out of the community was by boat, and the ships, the captains, the officers and men who manned them were the friends of everybody in town.

Captain John Andrew Cates, who had risked all in pioneering the Howe Sound run with his little steamer *Defiance* rapidly added to his fleet, until the Terminal Steam Navigation Company grew to considerable size. From the Furry, Boscowitz and Syndicate days until 1921 when he sold out to the Union Steamship Company, Captain Cates' little steamers were the sole link the mine had with the world beyond the mountains.

After the *Defiance* came *Britannia*, built in 1902 at False Creek, and from the Canadian Pacific Navigation Company, the forerunner to the Canadian Pacific Railway's coastal steamer service, he bought the *City of Nanaimo*, the *R.P. Rithet* and the *Joan*, renaming them *Bowena*, *Barramba* and *Ballena*. The *Bowena*, named after Bowen Island where Captain Cates had considerable land holdings, was subsequently known as the *Cheam* after she passed into the hands of the Union Steamship Company at the time of the merger. These notable old-timers were followed by the well-beloved "picnic boats" of the Union fleet, the *Capilano* and the Lady's, *Alexandra*, *Cecilia*, *Rose*, *Cynthia* and *Evelyn* which would arrive at the Beach wharf about noon, then go to Squamish and arrive back at the Beach at three, arriving in Vancouver at supper time. Thus a trip to town took all of 24 hours, whereas today, it's only a run of an hour or so.

These red and black funnelled ships, which called in at Bowen, Gambier, Woodfibre and Squamish, were fun to travel on. There was always somebody aboard who could play the piano and a rousing song-fest was the rule in the mahogany-lined salon, or if the weather was particularly fine, out on the deck.

And, of course, there were the captains, and everybody had their favorites, one of whom was Captain W.L. "Billy" Yates, master of the Lady Alex. Captain Yates was an old-time blue water man, whose career at sea began in 1901 as a cadet aboard the *Indefatigable*, which, shades of HMS *Britannia*, had been one of lord Nelson's flagships. He arrived on this coast in 1907 and died in Vancouver in 1966.

Not only was Britannia isolated from Vancouver, but communication between the camps was often difficult. Take the case of John Malm, who, in 1911, was working for the Goldsmith Copper Company at the Daisy Camp. In his diary he had this to say about hiking down to the Beach to pick up the mail:

January 22: Fell about two feet of snow for the last 24 hours. I went down to the Beach. A damned hard tramp in the snow.

January 27: Snowing as good as ever. I am walking up and down the hill to try to keep the trail open.

August 22: Very heavy thunder and rain, worst I ever seen on the Pacific Coast. Was down to the Beach. Got a good soaking before I got home.

November 16: Went to the Beach to bid Leaches' farewell. Had a good time while there but it was something else to climb the hill in the rain and snow.

Everything came up the winding trail. Pack horses brought in the heavy boxes of powder and everything which was too heavy to pack on the backs of humans; Japanese laborers hauled most of the supplies, and nobody, but nobody ever returned from the Beach to the mines empty handed. It was a good three hour hike, in either direction, so nobody took an "excursion" to the Beach lightly. As time went on, easier methods of communication were devised: the incline railway being the most important, but the aerial tramway, for freight only, and in some cases the surface and mine railways, served the most isolated, more or less bachelor communities.

The incline, or as it was more commonly – and affectionately – called "the skip", was the lifeline between the Beach and the Townsite, and it was one of Britannia's most famous tourist attractions. Passengers on the boats would get off and stay over until the boat came back from Squamish and Woodfibre, a matter of a couple hours. With great excitement they would gaily walk across the Beach Townsite to The Steps, and pause to think of the foolishness going somewhere to get nowhere. Was it worth it? Before boarding the skip at the power house level, a long flight of steps had to be faced, and whether or not they realized it, there were exactly 347 steps to take up, and therefore, 347 steps to come down. The faint hearted and the non-adventurer, gave up and returned to the dock to patiently await the return of the boat.

The skip was raised and lowered by a hoist situated at the head of the incline. One speed only – dead slow. (The official speed was 7½ miles per hour.) Two bare wires paralleled the track and these could be "shorted" by the brakey to signal the hoistman. Gravity powered sleds were also used for one way, single rider, trips by service workmen, the Doctor on emergency, small boys when undiscovered. Manual brakes controlled the speed and their use or non use could result in terrifying bursts of speed.

Surprisingly enough, there were very few accidents on the skip, in fact, only two of any consequence, and there were no fatalities in either of them. In the late 1930s an empty skip went wild, and came hurtling down the track at an incredible rate of speed, narrowly missed a group of children and then crashed into the mill. Again, lady luck was ruling Britannia that day, for some men who had been working at the very spot the skip crashed into, had left minutes before for lunch. For a while it was thought that one of the youngsters had been killed by the rampaging skip, but after the camp had been alerted of the "tragedy" and a search was made for his body, he was found, fast asleep, at home. The other occasion was when an operator, who was not familiar with the skip, having been a train man, used up all his air in the first few minutes of the trip, and as he got up speed found the brakes wouldn't work. Before the wayward skip was brought under control, several of the passengers leaped from the vehicle, and some received severe injuries, but those who stayed with it, panic stricken as they were, came out of the ordeal with nothing more than a severe case of fright.

From the top of the incline, the next step was to hop the narrow gauge mine train which passed right through the centre of the townsite, in fact, the tracks were the Main Street. Besides passengers the train carried freight, such as firewood and groceries, which were left at the nearest point to the consignee's house. In the case of the firewood, the pieces of cordwood would be too heavy to carry, so they were rolled down the hill, an operation which could be quite tricky. For instance: suppose a big log, rolling down the hill got out of control and went pell-mell on its way, what was to stop it from ploughing through flower gardens, vegetable patches and basement windows? Oh, it happened all right, but the canny townsiters soon took good care to see that this didn't happen very often. They put up little "wing dams" which altered the rolling logs down the paths and as a result seldom had difficulty. But when the logs did go off the beaten path, the ensuring mayhem was often unspeakable.

Travelling on the aerial tramway was, of course "verboten" and if anybody did take a trip on it, it was certainly not with the blessings of the safety men nor the management. However, a Japanese, remembered today as Chickasowa, did and nearly came to grief. He had made a bet with another Japanese that he could cross the valley, just below the townsite, by holding on to a bucket with his hands. And, without the knowledge of the operator, proceeded to prove his point. But before he got to the other side, the operator decided to call it a day and left the poor Japanese literally up in the air with no place to go but down, and down was a long way. And down Chickasowa went, and probably, much to his surprise as anybody else's, he survived. His days of heavy work, packing in supplies and doing manual labor, were over and the company put him to work running the pig pen and looking after chickens at Halfway. Hence the name Chickasowa.

The mine railway was probably one of the most unique railways in Canada. The operating signs were all bilingual, not French and English, but English and Japanese, thanks to J.W.D. Moodie.

The Japanese had come into the camp very early in the mine's history as surface laborers, packers and trackmen. At the Beach they had their own community on the north side of Britannia Creek, another at the Halfway and, at the lower portion of the Townsite, later known as Knobb Hill. The story goes that the white operators used to like to goof off and let the Japanese run the locomotives, without of course, any authorization from the office. One day Moodie made a visit to the mine and to his surprise found things not the way they should have been. With his famous blunt speech, "Pack up and get the next boat," ringing in their ears the white workers trekked down to the pier and the Japanese remained on the job. This was highly satisfactory to Moodie because he didn't have to pay the "High" wages the white workers earned and a penny saved was a penny earned.

Perhaps the most famous Japanese in the camp was Skookum, a mighty man was he, with long arms that seemed to stretch or as one resident put it, Skookum looked like an ape with clothes on. Skookum could carry a tremendous load on his back, and it was not uncommon to see him packing three 100-pound bags of concentrates with no apparent effort on his part. Like the rest of his countrymen he lived frugally and saved his money for a trip back home to Japan. When he had saved sufficient money he set out from his home at the lower Townsite for the Beach to take the boat to Vancouver where he intended to board one of the sleek white CPR "*Empress*" boats for Yokohama. Alas, somewhere between the Townsite and the Beach, Skookum lost his wallet containing all his money and tickets and the long awaited trip to Japan had to be cancelled.

Around 1925 settlement began at Minaty Bay, Hugh Chisholm's home is now on the site of one of the two original shacks at the Bay. At first the only way to get to the Bay was by boat. Building materials were put on scows and towed down, and the same methods had to be employed to bring the groceries to the several families who took up company-owned land here. During the winter months when gales blew up and down the Sound, this could be quite a hazardous operation.

A trail was ultimately put in the Beach to allow the isolated Minaty Bay residents to join in the social activities which went on at the Beach and at the Townsite, and it was far from being an extraordinary sight to see the ladies riding into town on bicycles, with their long dresses tucked up to keep them from getting caught in the chains. In 1944, a road was put in and supplies were brought in by the company truck.

About the same time, a waterworks system was put in and the wells and the little houses with half moons on the door went out of business. One of these little houses, however, continued to do yeoman service after it had been "de-holed". It became the local telephone booth.

At the far end of the Beach, a trail had been built to Phantom Lake, popularly known as Browning Lake, where C.P. Browning had a summer cottage which, when not in use by his family, was available to mine employees. The easiest way to get there, however, was by boat up the Sound, and then from the landing, a short walk took you to the Browning place. This property was eventually purchased by the B.C. Electric for their high tension power right of way and on the shores of the lake the provincial government had created the Murrin picnic grounds, a popular stopping place on the road to Squamish.

Part of Britannia's isolation from the rest of the world was broken in 1947 when a road was built linking Squamish with the Beach. It could be likened to a road which began nowhere and went nowhere, for with the exception of the PGE line to Quesnel, Squamish was just as isolated as Britannia. The new road, however, was preferable to the old water-route, particularly when the Squamish winds were blowing. As a result, the people at the Beach had one over the people at the Townsite: they could have cars and drive somewhere, which was some kind of oneupsmanship which the Townsite couldn't beat. And so it was with unabashed enthusiasms that the Townsite residents read a special edition of the Townsite Reporter in 1951 which headlined "Beach-Townsite road assured!"

"Your Townsite Reporter," announced the paper, "has just confirmed the spectacular news that the Company will start the construction of a road link between the Townsite and the Beach immediately. This First Special Edition of the Reporter tells the story behind this happy announcement."

The story quoted manager Cec. Roper as saying "The Mine surveyors have mapped out a proposed route which holds the grade down to approximately eight per cent for a road width of 16 feet and plan on surfacing the road with waste rock hauled out (of) the 2220 Level from development in the upper sections of the mine. The number of switchbacks have been kept to a minimum, even though there is a rapid rise in elevation. There are two costly bridges across Britannia Creek enroute and the entire link between the Beach and Townsite will have a total cost of well over one hundred thousand dollars."

"The cost of providing a road link to the Townsite," Mr. Roper said, "is so large that the approval for the money required for the construction cost was given only after the Company's Board of Directors were assured that independent transportation companies would provide regular passenger service to the Townsite for all commuters who do not own their own vehicles."

The road was completed the following year and the East Howe Sound Stage Company began a regular bus service between the two camps. As a result, the skip went out of business.

On March 25, 1954, Premier W.A.C. Bennett announced the Pacific Great Eastern Railway would be built from North Vancouver to Squamish, over the same route that Foley, Welch and Stewart had abandoned in 1913, and on August 27, 1956, at North Vancouver, C.R. Crysdale drove in a "last spike" made from copper from the Britannia Mine, and the first train from North Vancouver to Squamish rolled out of the spanking new yards.

At long last, Britannia's isolation was broken, and at the same time, a highway was literally being quarried along the shoreline of Howe Sound towards Squamish. On August 7, 1958, it was completed and a 600 car cavalcade led by Premier Bennett, passed through town.

Almost overnight the social life of the beach and the townsite began to suffer and slowly die. It couldn't compete with the attractions of the city which now were so close at hand.

Mount Sheer from Britannia Mountain, July 1944. BMM #13269

Aerial view of Mount Sheer, 1956. BMM #14152

Britannia Beach, 1960. BMM #14144

The Labour Rally at Britannia Beach, during the 1964-65 strike.
BMM #14076 (top) and 14074 (bottom)

Minaty Bay, 1966. BMM #14150

The PGE freight "Cannon Ball" rolling through Britannia, 1966. BMM #14141

A cabin at the old Daisy Camp, 1943. BMM #14151

Britannia Beach school, 1966. BMM #14143

Community Church, Britannia Beach, 1966. BMM #6221

10

LOOKING BOTH WAYS

Today the Townsite, or Mount Sheer, is far from being attractive place to visit. Where once there were rows of neatly kept homes, there are only gaunt rows of chimneys, ugly sentinels of a beautiful past. In the springtime, when the deep snow has given away, crocusses and snowdrops bloom, but there is nobody there to admire their beauty. And in the summer, other flowers, still in their once-kept beds, burst forth in a blaze of color and spread out to cover the wounds left by man. Few come to pick these flowers for an iron gate blocks the way. The Townsite sleeps.

But in the minds of many an ex-Britannia man and woman the old days are recalled with fondness and nostalgia, but few who lived in the Townsite wish to return to see it the way it is today. They prefer to remember it when it was "home", a happy place with a real community spirit. True, it was a company town, and like other towns in this category it had its good points and its bad. Some of these points the people wish to remember, and others they want to forget. They recall, with a deep longing for a return to the good old days when they paid the company a dollar a month per room for a comfortable home and the company took care of all the repairs. They recall the dances, the baseball games, and the self-made pleasures which were the products of their isolation from the bright lights and the sophistication of city life, not to say that life in the two communities at Britannia lacked any sophistication. Opening night at the theatre, for instance, was a formal occasion, and all the dances were long-dress affairs.

During the first couple of decades of life of the mine things, of course, were not as well organized as they were later on, but the company saw to it that plenty of recreational facilities were supplied, such as walks to Phantom Lake where the Browning's maintained a rustic summer home.

Closer to home was the beach, and in those days it was vastly different to what it is today. Then it was just as nature had created it, sandy, pleasant, but above all, clear of pollution. Everybody went there, except for one stretch known as Moodie's Beach and the reason this area was "out of bounds" is obvious. Some of the residents had their own boats which they pulled up on the shore, and to those who objected to Moodie's temperance laws, but still craved a week drap, these little crafts were the answers to a drinking man's prayer, for once aboard one of these "mercy ships" it was only a matter of, perhaps an hour at the longest, before a worshipper at the shrine of Bacchus could perform his sudsey ritual at one of the two temples in Squamish, the Newport or the Squamish Hotels. Seldom, if at anytime, did a Britannia-based boat bound for Squamish go "in ballast".

Since those days the shoreline has changed beyond recognition, for waste from the concentrator had been dumped here, and a couple of ships have been sunk as breakwaters and in the process of time and milling have been covered up themselves. Such was the fate of Captain Cates' little *Ballena*, one of the pioneer boats in the Britannia Beach-Vancouver service. No company likes to hear the stigmatic word "pollution" thrown at them, but it is, with or without significance, a fact that the biggest fish caught in the Howe Sound area are plucked from the waters adjacent to Britannia.

Only one raised in the city would put any significance on these summertime activities. In small communities everywhere these self-made activities were the norm, and so were the winter activities enjoyed at Britannia. When the cold snap started, a level area would be flooded for ice skating and hockey and the Townsite and the Beach would be decorated with rows of snowmen and forts and snowballs would go flying through the air.

From all outward appearances, then, there was little difference between Britannia and other mining towns in British Columbia. But Britannia was a company town, where the company saw all, heard all and whose word was the law. This atmosphere is difficult, if not impossible to set down in black and white, one has to live under these conditions to appreciate the subtle and the not-so-subtle difficulties. Yet it must be understood, for it was the alpha and omega of life in Britannia, both at the Beach and up at the Townsite.

Until C.P. Browning took over the management of the mine there had been practically no close company-employee relations, and considering the times, of course, this is not surprising. Under Browning's direction improvements along this line began through the establishment of community clubs in the two townsites. These organizations were to be the backbone of community activity fostering everything from dramatics to sports as well as being the bulwark between the company and the staff. All employees became members, the dues were $1.00 a month, and even in those days when a dollar was worth a dollar, it was a bargain. The special activities put on by the clubs were only rivalled by those which the company sponsored. And what deals the company put on for the employees! There were parties at Christmas for the kids, another at Halloween – which brings us to one of the mysteries of life which only a few can solve, and they aren't talking. It seems that sometime in the early 1930s the company threw a Halloween party, complete with ducking for apples, fireworks, costumes, etc., that a strange thing happened. And when morning's grey dawn arrived a strange, remarkable and puzzling sight greeted the people who dwelt at the Beach. As though a miracle had hit the town, the heavy iron and wood store delivery cart was observed hanging from the flagpole. The perpetrators of the interrogation in the Beach school was intense, but despite the grilling the culprits received, they remained silent, and the answer to the question as to how the cart got up there, is one of those mysteries whose answer is known only to God and the perpetrators, and neither are telling.

The company entered into their functions with enthusiasm, supplying the Santa Claus for the Christmas party and an unnamed gentleman on the executive level was ideally suited for the role. Consider also the wartime fair which the ladies of the Red Cross Corps arranged. The piece de resistance which made all the ladies swoon was the "Wild Man from Borneo". So fierce was he, yet so handsome, that Ringling Brothers should have grabbed that boy, although it might have been a bit difficult, for the "Wild Man" was the mill super. Yet such was his charm (in the costume) that if he had charged a dollar a kiss, the Red Cross Corps would have made a fortune.

Through the community clubs at the Beach grew the most enduring of all Britannia traditions, the Copper Queen. The first of these celebrations was held in 1925, the year after the forming of the club. At first the Copper Queen was elected through the community buying tickets, but this method was found to be grossly unfair and it was decided to elect a Queen through the school student body. On the 24th of May 1926 Thelma McKenzie was crowned Copper Queen and a crown, made from locally-produced red copper, fashioned by Armstrong Lowther, was placed on her head while other school children danced gayly around the Maypole. Through all the years, the good and the bad, this ceremony has continued to be one of the top events in the mining camp.

LIST OF COPPER QUEENS - BRITANNIA BEACH

1926 Thelma McKenzie, 1927 Pearl Russell, 1928 Elizabeth Jackson, 1929 Lena Fraser, 1930 Emily Browning, 1931 Agnes Madore, 1932 Kathleen McKenzie, 1933 Enid Davis, 1934 Doris Wharton, 1935 Mabel Clark, 1936 Lila Adamson, 1937 Mildred Bacon, 1938 Verna Phillips, 1939 Margaret Welby, 1940 Edith Newberry, 1941 Georgina Roach, 1942 Eleanor-Ann Matheson, 1943 Eleanor Jean Dunbar, 1944 Eloise Green, 1945 Jackie Donohue, 1946 Patsy Sullivan, 1947 Pat Hurley, 1948 Faye Settle, 1949 Sheila Fleming, 1950 Nancy Hill, 1951 Elizabeth Vollans, 1952 Olga Nicholson, 1953 Carol McLeod, 1954 Christine Adams, 1955 Winnifred Roper, 1956 Norma Adams, 1957 Marlene Anderson, 1958 Betty Bradley, 1959 Barbara Goss, 1960 Marlene Newell, 1961 Karen Lindley, 1962 Brenda Fleming, 1963 Edeltraud Beer, 1964 Karen Lindley, 1965 Brenda Fleming, 1966 Judy Fleming.

A year after the first Copper Queen was crowned down at the Beach the Townsite community club began their annual celebrations which were to be just as noteworthy as the one down at the Beach. Their big day was Dominion Day, July 1, and they also had a queen but the "succession" was not continuous, in fact only four girls wore the crown. They were Betty Lou Bogle, Joan Scott, Jacqueline Sanders and Linda Elliott.

Sports activities of all kinds were sponsored by the community clubs and leagues were formed between the Beach and the Townsite, and often with Woodfibre and Squamish. In this field in particular, the rivalry between the Beach and the Townsite was intense because it provided a visible outlet to the age old rivalry between the mill and the mine. Put simply this rivalry can best be expressed this way. Because of its location the mine always looked down on the mill, while the mill, in one sense and one sense only, had to look up to the mine, a patently unreasonable fact of life which the mine never let the mill forget, but which the mill folk had to endure. This inter-camp rivalry showed itself regularly, but once during the 1920s it reached the comic opera stage. The Beach baseball team was being clobbered left, right and centre field by the Townsite team and the losers began to despair of ever winning as much as a single game. Then the mill superintendent, had a brain wave. He slipped down to Seattle and hired a bunch of ball players from the University of Washington and put them to work in the mill. The results of the next game were magnificent, at least as far as the Beach was concerned.

The Townsite really couldn't call "foul", for after all, the new players *did* work at the mill and it was just the good fortune of the Beach that they happened to be ball players.

After their second straight defeat the Townsite came to the realization that the tide had turned and the people from the lower region might just take the season. Taking a page form the Beach book, the mine superintendent went down to Vancouver and hired a new crew of miners, who just happened to be ball players, and to the horror of the Beach fans, their newly found idols struck out. There was no joy that night at the Beach, and like the Townsite, they too had to snuff out any desire to shout "foul". It is unimportant to chronicle which team came out on top as such things are better left unsaid.

Sometimes baseball could be expensive for the Townsite club. Perhaps this is attributable to the brawn of the miners, but fly balls used to sail over the fence and into the creek, and one year the annual tab for baseballs came to $1000.

Basketball, too, was popular and each shift would have its own team. During the winter months boxing matches were held in the gym with some of the best pugilistic talent in Vancouver coming up either to put on exhibition matches or work in the mine.

With justifiable pride the twin communities could point to another contribution the community clubs made to the recreational facilities of Britannia. And they could also point out, with glee, to the people of Squamish, that though they might have the Pacific Great Eastern Railway, stores and two pubs, there were two swimming pools down at Britannia. The first of these, at the Beach, was put in in 1927 and the one up at the Townsite in 1930.

For their dollar a month dues the members also had full use of the library which was stocked with the latest and best books on the market, as well as a vast variety of newspapers, many in foreign languages, which kept the miners from abroad in contact with the news from back home.

Under the direction of the community clubs, the two camps had their own mimeographed newspapers, which, among other things, listed the latest books in the library, a column or two of comment, a social and personal column, weddings, as well as notices of upcoming events. These papers had a forerunner, a handsome little monthly magazine published "with the co-operation and assistance of the employees of the Britannia Mining and Smelting Company Ltd." Which, with P.A. Langerquist as editor, made its debut in February 1930. It lasted only six months.

A contest had been held earlier to name the paper. Some suggestions were Broanniaks and Copperation, but the winning name, suggested by Alan MacDonnell, of the Beach was "Britco News". The columns of this monthly contained a lot of whimsy, like the Sports Note from the Victoria Camp:

"Victoria is feeling pretty low after the exhibition they made against the Copper Plant. We had an idea that we had a fair team and would stand a good chance against anything the Townsite might produce. However, we aren't so sure now. From start to finish, Victoria made bonehead plays, the climax being reached when we allowed the Copper Plant to make a triple play on a series of asinine errors. Frank Hay claims it was the most pitiful game of ball he has ever umpired. But, Victoria can and will play good ball. Even the Yankees hit a slump sometimes."

In that same issue, May 1930, it was announced under Townsite Topics, "The talkies will be in operation at Britannia during the first week in June. With the talkie attachments, a new projector has been ordered for the Beach theatre. It is hoped that everyone will cooperate to make this new community venture a success. The least we can do is to make sure that we are not late."

There was also this tidbit from the Barbara Camp: "The Barbara Garbage Degenerating Plant, to give it its full title, dates its existence from shortly after the erection of the present camp buildings. To one familiar with the present modern and commodious structure, to one who has wandered through its spacious rag and bone department, and admired the deft-fingered Orientals in the rusty can and old boot section, and marveled at the up-to-date pie crust crusher, it is almost laughable to recollect that the original installation consisted of an ordinary municipal ashcan, the contents of which were disposed of by the simple expedient of emptying of the Empress Camp. The overhead conveyor system is an important feature and has been worked without a breakdown for the last seventeen years since some unknown hero suggested greasing the pulley. The present equipment was supplied by the Wun Lung Superfluity Carbonization Company of Hong Kong, China."

Again from the Barbara, we find this note: "The cat-catching squad recently has been increased to four men and seven dogs, all on special rations of a wide nutritive ratio conducive to extreme activity. The depredations due to cats are now inconsiderable. It is said of the Plant Manager, to illustrate his close contact with affairs, that he can tell almost immediately if a cat has visited the premises."

And back at the Victoria, there was a smoker, which in itself was not unusual, but the Britco News correspondent says this one, held on March 29, 1930 "was really good." It began with a First Aid Competition and when this was over, the party began. The men came up from the Townsite with their band and they came from the Empress as well, and here's what happened.

"The Shifters were called upon to sing, but only Bill Ivey and Jimmy Deas would face the music. We believe they sang "Carry Me Back to Old Virginy" with gestures. The gestures were quite good.

"Bill Dawson, our whispering baritone, sang a couple of delightful selections and started on another, but his throat became dry and he had to stop. We think he sang again later.

"Mr. Clarke and his neighbor each received a piece of banana shortcake down the neck.

"Without a doubt Andy McIntosh was the hit of the evening. He led the band, step danced, sang, boxed a few rounds with Jimmy Deas, made whoopee generally, and finally disappeared behind the piano."

The ladies, too, had their functions, at which tea was poured and it was very, very genteel:

"The Summer festival given by the Beach Ladies Aid," said the News in July, "attracted a large attendance. The booths were sold out early and there was very little left on the refreshment tables towards the end. The fortune teller worked overtime gratifying the curiosity of those who wished to peer into the future. Among the entertainment numbers, Mrs. Sybil Munroe's Spanish dance and her sister Cleo's classic and hornpipe dances delighted the spectators. Mrs. Green should be pleased with the performance of her pupils Buddy Munroe, Winnie McGaw and Miss E. Bagshawe. Mrs. W. Louther accompanied by Mrs. A. Hewson, rendered two solos. A dance wound up the evening."

The townsite, too, could put on a hop with éclat. "The Firemen's Ball this year (they began in 1927) came on March 28. Skip Richardson, assisted by Paul Snider, contrived a clever decorative scheme for the gym through the use of Pyrene extinguishers, fire fighting equipment and original signs draped with flags. Geordie Scott handled the dance with his usual savoir faire. Close to the door Mr. Moore, acting as host on behalf of the Company, and wondering if he shouldn't have stayed at home, because Mrs. Moore was in California." (James Moore, mine superintendent left in June 1930 to be general manager of the Chelan Copper Mining Company, another subsidiary of the Howe Sound Company.)

The little notes carried in the Britco News even now, more than 35 years after they were first published, make interesting reading:

"Bill Beaton, whose hirsute decorations were the pride and envy of the entire camp, was compelled to remove the disguise owing to an unexpected visit of friends.

"The long evening dresses worn by the ladies at the Firemen's Ball looked a little strange at first, but they were very becoming and covered a multitude of shins.

"The lantern slides at Victoria Camp are greatly enjoyed, although some of the boys think that a few slides of Clara Bow would be acceptable."

And jokes: "Did you hear the one about the one-eyed Scotsman who tried to get into the Barbara theatre for half price?" The Britco news also tells of a visit of a then up-and-coming boxer, 22 year-old Jimmy McLarnin, who was soon to meet Young Jack Thompson for the second time. "Jimmy's right hand has a swelling the size of an egg which he received when he fractured his hand in the last fight against Thompson. We hate to think of what Jimmy is going to do to Thompson with two fists when he has won a decision while his right hand was useless. Yet – with all that, Jimmy is a nice, well-spoken chap and he went over big with the big boys." Three years later, in May 1933, Jimmy McLarnin became world welterweight champion.

The end of the Britco News came in July. The price of copper dropped to 11 cents, the lowest since 1914, and as we have seen, long days of trial lay ahead. The end was announced in these words: "The publication of the Britco News will be discontinued for the time being." Another tombstone had been laid to the memory of a B.C. mining camp journal.

But before leaving the Britco News, we must not forget the Laird of South Valley who contributed to the magazine. The Laird was Armstrong "Slim" Lowther, Britannia's poet laureate. Lowther had begun work as a blacksmith about 1914 and later became watchman up at the South Valley dam. Life up there was lonely and it was during this time that he composed a great number of poems which were subsequently privately printed in a book entitled, "Poems by Laird", which he gave to his friends. Mrs. Lowther, the former Winifred Carden, was a music teacher and was active in many organizations down at the Beach. The Laird died in 1948.

For the next 20 years, after the Britco News folded, there was a void in the journalistic life of Britannia.

If a local paper had been published the activities it could have reported on would have been boundless. It could have told us, of the winter of 1933 when 35 feet of snow fell on the Townsite, or it might have explored Bert Hamilton's bear story.

As he was the sole witness to this event, his story of the three bears cannot really be refuted. But he claimed that one day there were two bear cubs in his pantry up at the Townsite. They were helping themselves to all the goodies inside, dropping them out the window to mother bear who was so large she couldn't get in the house.

Bears were fairly common up at the Townsite and save for the knocking over of garbage cans they were little or no trouble, although when they were around, mothers of young children would keep the tads indoors just in case the bears decided to earn a new reputation. Some of the bears like those who used to hang around the Empress camp were treated like pets, and great was the indignation when a hunter from Squamish shot them. Said the correspondent to the Britco News: "Our bears, the ones we fed and tamed, have left. Two of them have been murdered and the rest have gone in search of healthier localities. They were quite harmless. Commercially their hides were no good. They afforded us considerable amusement. They saved the bull-cook a great deal of firing in the incinerator, and yet the poor unsuspecting animals were slaughtered within a few minutes of being fed.

"One does meet those people who cannot see a wild animal without wanting to shoot it; but if the animals were equally equipped it might be another story. They should have gone to the last war, where they would have discovered, as many of us have, that after chasing and being chased by the other fellow, there is very little kick to be found in the shooting of harmless and defenceless animals."

In March 1949 the Townsite Community Club began publishing the Townsite Reporter (subsequently the Mount Sheer Reporter) and the following January the Beach Community Club turned out the first issue of their Journal, The Beachcomber. Both these little mimeographed monthly's lasted until the camp closed down. In 1963 another paper, sponsored by the Britannia Community Club, the Beach Monthly, came into existence. It later became the Britannia News.

These journals tell us a lot about the activities in the communities they served and when put altogether the number of organizations active in Britannia during that decade is quite impressive. In fact, in 1954, the annual report of the Howe Sound Company reflected this activity in these words: "It is becoming a very real problem to find dates that do not conflict."

Amongst the organizations whose activities were covered by the two papers are: First Britannia Wolf Pack, the Scout Troop, Brownie Pack and Guide Pack; Mt. Sheer Branch of the Royal Canadian Legion, Post No. 186, which was located at the Beach, the Parklane Branch, up at the Townsite; the East Howe Sound Overture Association, made up of members from both communities as well as Squamish and Woodfibre; the Credit Union; Parent-Teacher's Association; the various union, school and church organizations, such as the Ladies Auxiliary to the union, the Catholic Women's Guild, Community Church Ladies Aid, the C.G.I.T. and the North Star Explorers.

While there had been a good deal of church activity at both the Townsite and the Beach, the work had been handicapped by the lack of adequate buildings and time. From the earliest days of the mine, Methodist and Presbyterian mission boats made Britannia more or less a regular port of call. Roman Catholic priests also visited the camp, as did Anglican and Lutheran clergy. A Protestant church had been established up at the Townsite with the company providing a house for a manse, with the minister attending to the spiritual requirements of both communities.

However it was not until June 1952 that a $16,500 church was erected at the Beach by voluntary labor. This church was officially opened on April 19, 1953 and it must be one of the most unique in Canada, for both Protestant and Roman Catholic services are held under the same roof, although at opposite ends of the building, and separated by a wall. The Church at Mount Sheer has been closed since February 28, 1958.

The Women's Association of the Protestant Church, founded on September 30, 1926 up at the Townsite, began what was to be one of the most popular pastimes in the Townsite. From almost the first, they put on dramatic events, and this ultimately, though not directly, led to the founding, in 1942 of the Britannia Townsite Players Club. Leading lights in the organization were L.G. Stewart, M. Knight, C. Freemand, Betty Trythall, L. Bjorkman, C.G. and Brownie Sherriff, and Wesley Black.

In 1946 the group entered the B.C. Regional drama festival, submitting the play the Legend. In covering this event, the *Vancouver Sun* noted that adjudicator Owen J. Thomas criticized the performance for "inconsistency of pace" but praised Mrs. Sherriff for the "outstanding character performance of the evening."

The following is a list of some of the plays produced by the players' club: Sherlock Holmes, Jr.; The Lucky Seventh; The Family Upstairs; Which is the Way to Boston?; Sleeping Dogs; The Bishop of Munster; Jacob Comes Home; Look Me in the Eye; The Ghost Train; Out of the Frying Pan; Arsenic and Old Lace; Courage, Mr. Green; I'm a Fool; Last Flight Over; The Woman in Budapest; Suds in Your Eye; The Green Vine; The Festered Lily; Father of the Bride.

In addition to this troupe, the High School also had its theatre company, for these, the curtain has rung down for the last time, the lights are turned off.

There are many tales about Britannia which are told around the coffee cups whenever two or three Townsiters or Beachers get together. They present all kinds of problems to the historian; where to fit them into the running text, and, in some cases, whether to believe them or not. Anyway, they deserve to be retold and preserved, for they are the stories which people remember, and have become part of the folklore at Britannia.

Seated around the coffee table in the general offices one day, the talk centered around a gentleman by the name of Gorman, a Canadian Industries Ltd. Explosive salesman who should have known better. One day, his last in the mine, he came to the property ill-equipped for walking through the wet portal sets of the 1050, so he picked up a sheet of galvanized iron to hold over his head to keep the water off. It obstructed his vision, and he walked into an oncoming locomotive. Exit Mr. Gorman.

Animal stories, too, are often told, including the one of the intrepid hunter, Phil Butters. On this occasion the game was goat, and the one he shot rolled down the mountain side to the creek where it lay cold dead. It was a beautiful specimen, so Phil laid down his rifle and went to get a closer look at his trophy. Bre'r Goat, however, still had life in him, eyed Mr. Butters with a mean look, and tried to get up. Butters happened to have a Bowie knife with him, and helped the goat to depart from this vale of tears.

Then there was Bowser, the dog who loved to ride the skip. One day while waiting outside the store for the skip to leave, he sat by the track dusting it with his tail. Suddenly the skip began to move, and Bower and his tail severed connections.

We have, in earlier pages, chronicled stories of the bears at Victoria Camp. Here is another as a reminder to keep in close contact with companions when hunting. Take the case of Charles Sherriff and Fred Haig berry picking near Victoria Camp. Mr. Sherriff became a little peeved at the way Mr. Haig was acting. He was, Mr. Sherriff declared, shaking the bush he was working on, and it wasn't very nice of him. There was no response from the other side, so Mr. Sherriff, parted the bush to tell Mr. Haig face-to-face to desist. And there, glaring at him, was not Mr. Haig but a bear!

Mine Superintendent J.I. Moore brought in some cows and chickens, and was much puzzled by the fact that they were not as productive as they might have been. A little detective work showed that the rail crews stopped to milk the cows and swiped the eggs. He also lost a pig which turned up at a barbecue. However miners are not necessarily chefs, and the details of barbecuing were completely unknown, or at best ignored, so the pig had finally to be snuck into the cookhouse where the Chinese chef, after much protesting finished the job.

Sam Perkins, troubled with civet cats in his basement made the mistake of trying to get rid of them with a shotgun. The civet cats remained but left a message. He then called for help from an electrician. A system was rigged up for dangling copper wire from the trolley wire. The 600 volts generated didn't kill the animals either just infuriated them. Dora's fur coat, hanging in the basement was never the same again.

Back at the Victoria Camp, the scene of so many good stories, the tale is told of Fred Hornton's Christmas tree. Just before the Yuletide visit to his home in Vancouver. Mr. Hornton carefully selected a fir tree, hauled it into the mine, up the shaft, out of the mine, onto the skip, down the steps, onto the boat, protected it enroute, then off the boat, into a streetcar (after some argument with the conductor), then transferred to another car, (another argument) and so he reached home, proud but worn out and in no mood for the critical appraisal given the tree by his wife. This took the form of six words which cut through to the marrow: "That's not much of a tree," she said, and went on with her dinner preparations. Mr. Hornton did a slow burn, his face was likened unto a technocolor movie, but not a word did he say.

Instead, he picked up a hatchet and cut the poor little tree into pieces and threw it into the furnace. Later in the evening his wife asked when he was going to set up the tree. Mr. Hornton barely looked up from his newspaper, and merely answered, "What tree?" and returned to his reading.

Perhaps, under a situation like that, he should have had some of Bob Dick's grape juice. To his special customers and friends at the store he sold a special Concord grape juice which was carefully spiked at a ratio of one quart of rum for every 10 gallons of juice. Although many unsaleable types of merchandise at the store were raffled, it is not recorded that any of Bob Dick's special grape juice ever remained on the shelves long enough to be classed unsaleable.

The telephone system was the source of many stories. It wasn't the nosiness of the other members on the party line but the operators that was amazing. Every call had to go through the operator. If you phoned Mrs. Smith the operator might let the phone ring a couple of times and then come back on the line with "I don't think she's there. Mrs. Brown phoned her this morning. She's probably over there having coffee" or "Oh she's not at home. Both Blacks and Greens are having a party tonight. I'm sure they were invited to Blacks. Just a minute and I'll call over there."

One of the boys calling his wife from the mine got the wrong number. He called back to the operator. She insisted she'd made no mistake. "But you must have," said Charlie, "a man answered and there's no man there!" "You can never tell," replied the operator as she dialed again.

Now there was a breed of men in town, on whom it might be said the full wrath of Mr. Moodie would have descended had that worthy been around. The story tellers have left us only one name in connection with this tale and it is "Hardrock" Johnson.

Mr. Johnson was engaged one night in a bout of poker with another gentleman, who it turned out, was temporarily financially embarrassed. He promised to go out and get the money owing right away, but after a decent interval had passed, Mr. Johnson went to see what was holding him up. Outside, he spotted his creditor standing in a doorway, but instead of a fistful of money, he was holding a revolver. There was a loud "BANG" but fortunately, the only damage caused was a hole in Mr. Johnson's hat. The majesty of the law thereupon descended upon the gunman, and Britannia's only recorded gunslinger fades from history without even his name being known. *Sic transit gloria.*

One of the big attractions at the bi-weekly movie was the color provided by George Mitchell. He never failed to put on a show of his own. It began when he stood in front of the hall and bellowed "last call" in such good voice that he could be heard right through the town. Then he entered the hall and kept order till the movie began. If the children up front were restless his "Sit down ye little prespbyterians" in stentorian tones soon settled them down. When it was time for the show to start he invariably walked down the aisle and shouted "Let'er goooooooo" – though the projectionists in their isolated box couldn't hear him and just hoped their watches were synchronized. If the film broke – as frequently happened – Geordie was right there in the aisle announcing to all and sundry that "There is something wrong with the technicality."

Geordie loved to exaggerate. If his roof leaked it was the worst leak in town. Why, his wife had to cook his dinner in a sou-wester.

And finally, we have the reminiscences of a Townsite.

"For two months of the year – from the end of November till the end of January no sun reaches the valley. You've heard of sun worshippers. Every year, about the 24th of January, we joined the cult. Everybody was elated when the sun hit the first house and as every other day another one or two houses were bathed in light the progress of the sun became the chief topic of conversation and our spirits were lifted.

"Instead of getting rain in the winter we got snow – and more snow. And there was just no place to put it. The heaviest snowfall year I remember was when we got 35 feet. The walks to the houses had snow banks 10 feet high and many windows had to be boarded up to prevent the pressure of the snow from breaking them. A snow plow kept the skip track clear but the rest of the town had little more than trails. The snow usually lasted from Halloween till May.

"But though the Beach was commonly known as the Banana Belt the Townsite was still able to produce lovely gardens after the snow. Many of the homes here have been beautified by plants and shrubs removed from the Townsite after the shutdown and the prolific raspberries up there are still enjoyed.

"There was quite a pride taken in the homes. Originally all the ceilings were about 11 feet high and walls were all V-join. Many a decorating bee was held to lower ceilings or paper the walls; I don't think many alterations could have been made in the houses before 1940 because I know we moved three times and we covered the V-Join in three houses. It makes me tired just thinking about it.

"It was quite a procedure when anyone moved. One move regularly caused five others – sometimes more. Everybody would scramble after a better house – i.e. a house of the same original design but one which had more improvements made in it – the ceiling lowered, a partition moved or a lean-to added or a better garden. There were no moving vans of course or facilities for moving. Friends were rounded up who trundled the furniture up and down the hills and then a swinging party celebrated the occasion. I remember one girl, inexperienced in local moving who left everything in her refrigerator. Nobody thought to look inside. By the time the amateurs had it set up again in the new house – well, you never saw such a mess.

"When I arrived – as a bride – at the Townsite in 1940 there were three bunkhouses, a cookhouse and hotel, and about 200 families making a total population of about 1200. The men worked a six day, 48 hour week with three holidays – Christmas, New Years and July 1. Boxing Day was taken off too but the men "paid" for it by working the Sunday before Christmas. Three whistles woke the camp at 6:00, two whistles at 6:30, one at 5 to 7 and one at 7:00 when work started. There were no alarm clocks needed.

"There was a hospital – really little more than a first aid station but it did have a thriving maternity ward – a five room school with grades one to 12 (The Beach high school students commuted daily), a Protestant and Catholic church, a theatre offering two shows a week, a store and a clubhouse.

"The store sold groceries, meat, patent medicines, hardware and drygoods. The drygoods consisted chiefly of men's work clothes. Most of us shopped by catalogue. The service in the store – or lack of it – was unbelievable. We were a captive market and the supervisors were at the Beach. When old timers get together recollections of the store are a source of great merriment – but it wasn't so funny then.

"The drygoods department for instance, flatly refused to serve women after three o'clock. The pleas that you had to wait till your husband got home for a baby sitter made no difference. We'd have to go home and send our husband back for a spool of thread. The selling was anything but high pressure. It was definitely reluctant. The phrase, "Madam there's a war on" became almost a password in the town it was heard so frequently in response to the most ordinary request. Then there was a fire in the store and the fire sale that followed was a real eye-opener. Piles and piles of articles we'd been denied the privilege of buying and many things we'd never seen on the shelves – such as high button boots.

"It was quite a sight to see one of the grocery clerks 'making' bread, as he called it, every morning. Some of these horrible women you know felt the bread to see if it was fresh so he would gently knead the old bread every morning and then artfully disperse it among the fresh loaves. But the clerks had a lot to put up with too. We all had our idiosyncrasies.

"We never carried cash – though we did have bank service every two weeks. So at the store everything was charged and the store bill was taken off the check as a payroll deduction. Some wives who didn't appreciate their husbands playing poker every payday would make sure the store bill ate up all the cheque and frequently more than the cheque. As a consequence some of the men practically did "owe their soul to the company store."

"The Club House was the centre of a lot of activity. It had a big gymnasium where basketball, volleyball, badminton, wrestling and boxing matches and dances were held. It also housed a barber shop, poolroom, reading room, library committee rooms and a kitchenette which was open from 7 - 12 p.m. A year round recreation director was employed who handled the gym activities in the winter months and the swimming pool in the summer.

"It was an isolated camp. Britannia was only accessible by boat – a daily service. From Britannia we climbed the 347 steps – uncovered then incidentally – to the foot of the incline railway (now the 4100 parking lot). From there we boarded a cable car – which was an uncovered flat car and rode for 15 minutes standing at an angle of about 30 degrees, squeezed in between oil barrels, freight and other passengers. At the top of the incline we transferred to an electric railway for a 3½ mile trip that took half an hour.

"I think most of us went 'out' no more than two or three times a year. The six day week left the men little time for traveling. If the women got particularly bushed or completely frustrated with catalogue buying they could take the day trip. In the winter this meant boarding the skip at 7 a.m. in snowboots, winter coats, mitts, scarves, etc. and arriving in Vancouver at noon to find the sun shining or rain raining – in any case unsuitably clothed. There would be four or five hours of frantic shopping before catching the boat back. And when we finally staggered off the skip at 11 p.m. we had had it for another few months.

"How did we spend our time? Our problem was to find time for our housework. In the winter we played volleyball, basketball or badminton. The badminton was particularly attractive in that it provided us with some of the few outside contacts we had. We used to have round robin tournaments with the Beach, Squamish and Woodfibre. Outdoor toboganning and sledding were enjoyed by adults as well as children.

"After the snow left we played softball, tennis and swam. And summer and winter we hiked on the weekend – that is Sunday. We went to the ski cabin, to Pettgill Lake to skate or picnic, to the old Daisy Camp, to Mountain Lake. Occasionally we rode down to the Beach to hike to Brownings Lake (there was no road then) or we followed the pipeline to Phyllis and Marian.

"For indoor entertainment there was an endless round of teas, luncheons, card parties, etc. There were Book Clubs, a Square Dance Club, a Players Club. The award for the best actress in B.C. came to the Townsite one year. Every month the Club had a big formal dance – long dresses were a must. Can you see us walking between the snowbanks with our long dresses and overshoes, clutching our high heels and prepared to climb the bank if the skip came. We weren't so formal in other ways though. We never wore hats. Among one group a hat was passed around continually. That hat got to Vancouver many times – on a different head each trip.

"A Vancouver orchestra was always imported and for the big Burns Dance in January the Townsite went all out with bagpipes, haggis, etc. Another big dance was the Ladies Auxiliary to the Union's Rose Ball. Millions of paper roses were made for this and the gym was transformed. The Church was very active too – with dinners, bake sales, telephone bridges, social evenings and a yearly bazaar. We worked 11 months of the year on the Bazaar and one year cleared over 1200 dollars. Church work as other community activities got wholehearted support. Being a member of the Church or Club sponsoring the event just meant a little more responsibility. Practically every event was well attended probably because so many had worked so hard in the preparation of it.

"During the war almost every woman in town gave two full days a week to the Red Cross.

"We had no policemen at the Townsite and really no crime – other than bootlegging. There was little juvenile delinquency...perhaps due to the management's directive "Look after your kid or get out" or perhaps due to the fact that we were so close it was hard to get away with anything. There are no secrets in an isolated small town.

"By 1953 our isolation came to an end with the road to the Beach. A few cars appeared on the property. You could drive to Squamish and almost five miles beyond. Our close community life changed. The high school students commuted to Squamish for their education. The almost 100 percent support for local affairs ended with many preferring a beer in Squamish to a party in Mount Sheer. The trip to Vancouver was three hours shorter and much more comfortable and we made it much oftener.

"I was talking to an old friend of the Townsite. She said "Just tell them it was fun." "

All things must have an end and so our story draws to a close but not before we say a few words on what the future promises to Britannia and its people.

The note of sadness, with which the changing company structure and the effect of this change on the mine has been described, must alter to one of rising optimism in recounting this promise.

The Anaconda Company of more than 100,000 shareholders, some of them residents of Britannia, producers of 13% of the world's output of copper, employers of 45,000 men and women engaged in mining, smelting and manufacturing throughout the world had been looking for means of establishing exploration headquarters and research facilities in Western Canada. Britannia offered these means and, further, offered a producing mine as a source of revenue from which some of the expense of the search for new mines might be borne. With this producing mine, almost as a bonus, came a working force of men ready to do their part and share with the new management the benefit of their years of service and experience.

While it seemed, in the opinion of some observers, that Britannia's future had passed, it was a proven fact that all the orebodies had not "bottomed", that deeper down some of them were still open and that, given a lot of intelligent persistence in the search, another horizon of mineable ore was waiting to be found.

Anaconda has encouraged this intelligent persistence and the ore has been found.

As we close our story, structures true to the pattern of those from which Britannia has yielded its wealth in the past, are being evolved. Day to day the drills draw core from the deep holes and the picture of the mine's future clears. Britannia's future is to be a bright one, bountiful and beneficial to many for years to come.

Community Club, Britannia Beach, 1966. BMM #6230

Britannia Beach Hospital, 1966. BMM #6212

The Store, Britannia Beach, 1966. BMM #6208

General offices, Anaconda Copper Company, Britannia Beach, 1966. BMM #6223

Research laboratory, Britannia Beach, 1966. BMM #6222

Copper precipitation plant (launders), Britannia Beach, 1968. BMM #6218

Ritz Bunkhouse, Britannia Beach, 1966. BMM #6231

Pyrite Plaza apartments, Britannia Beach, 1966. BMM #6211

"Shaughnessy Heights" above the Townsite at Britannia Beach, 1966.
BMM #6210

Britannia Beach, 1966. BMM #6217

Mine buildings at Britannia Beach, 1966. BMM #6219

General view of Britannia Beach, 1966. BMM #6220

The highway to Squamish. BMM 11734

2004 EPILOGUE – From 2nd Edition

The one thing all Britannia Beach residents have in common is our love of the "Beach" and our desire to live here. We have enjoyed over the last 25 years the scenery, nature and quietness of our surroundings with a unique freedom from most urban rules. As people pass by on the Sea to Sky Highway most are unaware of our little community on the hillside.

In the early 80's a mobile home park was created above the houses. It sat almost empty for years. A mobile home sales outlet found us in the early 90's and soon most of the spaces were filled. After the flood all of the mobiles along the creek were encouraged to move off the flood plain to the park. More than one half of our resident population lives in mobiles.

Over the last 15 years or so if you are a TV buff or movie goer you may have seen Britannia Beach in the background as we have become a very popular location with the film industry. Many of our locals have been able to find employment with the movies and some are even trying to make a career of it.

Hope Island, a TV series found its home here in Britannia Beach. Their time here was very beneficial to our community. They spent nearly a year preparing sets using many locals. They built a replica of a church on the hillside and altered the miners bunkhouse "The Ritz" to look like a church as well as building the fishing village. The two churches used are visible reminders of Hope Island to this day. Tourists often stop to take pictures, thinking they are real historical sites. As a thank you, at the end of the second season they repaired the ball field that still had not come back from the flood.

When the show was cancelled it was a sad time, but we had a great time shopping as they sold off the props at better than bargain prices. They left the sets intact; this has added to the draw of Britannia as a movie set. Many celebrities have filmed here: Robin Williams, Leslie Nielson, and Malcolm Jamal Warner to name a few.

The Mining Museum has set in motion many innovative programs and exhibits making it a major tourist attraction. The community has complimented this, adding the small kiosks along the highway. It is a favoured stop of Tour bus lines, with world famous Fish & Chip take out, restaurant, coffee shop, general store and several gift shops making a pleasant break on the way to Whistler.

Our eclectic community has managed to be very innovative in job creation. We have several artisans, who create and craft, jewelry, art, stained glass and ceramics. Hundreds of tons of wild mushrooms are packed and exported from Britannia Beach with the help of the neighbourhood. Floral greens is also a thriving business in Britannia, supplying many lower mainland nurseries.

We've had some unfortunate losses and major disasters over the years! The original powerhouse burned when a poor little raccoon grabbed two wires causing an arc which started the fire. The abandoned hospital became the local teenage hangout and an abandoned candle sent that to the ground. The 4100 machine shop was a spectacular fire with all the heavy equipment burning. The old Prince George cruise ship became an addition to our community and met its demise due to a questionable fire which became a roadside attraction as it burned for 3 weeks.

The biggest catastrophe in the last twenty-five years was the huge flood in 1991. Britannia Creek deposited gravel four feet deep covering parked vehicles and flooding the lower community and highway. We pulled together during this time, with the aid of the Provincial Emergency Program, housing those displaced and helping wherever needed. At this time we lost the gas station, the general store and our footbridge.

Efforts to save the concentrator from deterioration are being made. It is our Britannia Beach landmark. When the movie industry lights it up at night it brings back a memory of its past glory.

Although it has not affected our health, our gardens or our relaxed way of life the acid rock drainage has been a significant player in the ownership of the property. Over the years, the property has changed hands many times. Each change has made for concern regarding our tenure.

Legislation implemented to address the problem of pollution has led to all past perpetrators of the acid rock damage contributing to cleanup which is 30% complete. In 2005, the limewater treatment plant will be operational.

Since the start of the cleanup our creek has lost most of the orange colour indicating pollutants. Barnacles are growing at the mouth.

Shore birds are returning in increasing numbers and we even had an orca "killer" whale visit Howe Sound in 2003. Can-oxy, the chemical plant at the head of the sound in Squamish is also cleaning up, improving the water quality of the sound.

With the guidance provided by the Charette sponsored by key community stakeholders we seem to be developing a common vision. We look forward to Britannia developing into the bustling community it was in earlier days.

I have very much enjoyed all the years I have lived here in Britannia. My flower garden is well established and provides me with many hours of enjoyment. My favourite hobby is my bee house with ten hives. All enjoy the delicious Britannia Beach blackberry honey, which I like to give away.

Betty Shore, resident of Britannia Beach

A MEMORY OF BRITANNIA BY JOAN EHLER, ORIGINAL MEMBER OF THE BRITANNIA BEACH COMMUNITY CLUB

Can I tell you the first time it really struck me that this place was gone? They decided in '74 to shut it down because it was costing too much to get the ore out and it wasn't profitable. And it took quite a while to mop everything up and get things out of the mine and that sort of thing. And one day I went to Squamish grocery shopping and when I came back the Mill, the concentrator, was dark. And I sat up on the bluff and I couldn't come home because I was crying so hard. It was the saddest thing, I had never seen the Mill building without lights in it, and that's when I knew it was over after being here for so many years.

As recorded on March 25, 2004.

2014 EPILOGUE

The 2004 Epilogue looked at some of the changes in residency and community over the years. Yet it is difficult to bring it up to date without briefly looking back again over the four decades after the closure of the Mine as doing this will give the last decade more context.

The tale of these four decades are worthy of a book in itself. The political wrangling of a community fighting for their survival was at times heart wrenching and at other times joyous. Those that stayed in Britannia Beach and Minaty Bay after the Mine closed found work locally either across Howe Sound at Woodfibre Pulp & Paper or in Squamish where BC Rail and the logging industry were still going full bore. By 1978, new families, mainly from Squamish, had moved in, drawn by the reasonable rent prices. It was a friendly community where still no one locked their doors and plenty of activities took place to entertain young and old alike. The elementary school still operated. There was an outdoor swimming pool, tennis courts, a ball field, dance hall and Community Club as well as a gas station, restaurant and store. The Post Office was the hub of the community as everyone went there daily to check the mail and there was always someone to chat with.

As time marched on, ownership switched to Copper Beach Estates in 1979. The wrangling increased as community members knew the town was in need of significantly more investment than was being made. Conflict of interest, receivership, court cases and decaying infrastructure all played a part in the community's story. The town still was, and still operated as, a Company Town. There remained no home owners, only tenants. And as was outlined in the previous pages, fire and flood again hit the community. Yet at the heart of all this were the residents who knew the community was worth saving. Artists, entrepreneurs, activists and lobbyists among others all made up the fabric of this little community.

A major turning point came around the turn of the Millennium. Ownership again changed hands, this time to Macdonald Development. Much of the mine site was transferred to the Province while Macdonald retained ownership of Britannia Beach and surrounding lands. The land transfer facilitated government control of the pollution remediation and in exchange Macdonald received permission to subdivide the residential properties. Along with a myriad of consultants, government was engaged to study the pollution issues and formulate a remediation plan. Reclamation work began throughout the site, work that is still ongoing.

The Developer proceeded over the next few years to create a plan that would allow existing residents right of first refusal to purchase their homes, fee simple at an affordable price. An additional 92 building lots were cleared and serviced for sale to the general public. In town, some of the heritage buildings including the facades of the old school, Honeymoon Suites, Clubhouse and bunkhouses were restored with an eye of developing a boutique style tourist attraction in close proximity to the waterfront and highway. In 2005 for the first time in Britannia's history, the lots were sold. Most of the existing residents were successful in purchasing their homes, a dream come true especially for those who had fought steadfastly for so long to stay there. Once again, new families moved in and continue to do so to this day. While the face of the Community has changed in some ways with the development of new roads and services and the building of large modern houses, there is a vibrancy that has also returned, harkening back to the 'old days' with the influx of a young enthusiastic generation. The streets are once again filled with the sounds of happy children.

Perhaps the most obvious change to the town came with the exterior rehabilitation of Mill 3, completed in 2007. With no maintenance after the closure of the Mine, the building had deteriorated to the point where it was in danger of being demolished for safety reasons. A $5 million investment from government grants, industry and individual donors allowed the building to be saved. It is once again a landmark. The Museum (formerly the BC Museum of Mining) underwent refurbishment and relaunched in 2010 as the Britannia Mine Museum.

In 2009, the Customs Shed and wharf, one of the town's more iconic structures was lost to the elements. Years previously it was under threat of being demolished through burning. This was averted thanks to the efforts of a few members of the community, yet the ravages of time eventually took its toll. It had become more and more dilapidated as time went on until finally a winter storm sent it into the drink one night.

For many years, the Britannia Beach Volunteer Fire Department has been an active member of the Community. They host the annual

Christmas Party for the kids followed by the Community Club's Pot Luck and Dance in the evening for the adults. The original Copper Queen throne (now part of the Museum's collections) is used for Santa each year, a tradition that goes way back. In 2010, the VFD moved into a purpose built Fire Hall and built a dedicated a space to serve as the proud new home to the historic 1951 Ford Mercury fire truck.

Regarding the pollution issue, going years back, it was the community that lobbied with government officials, bureaucrats, lawyers and anyone who would lend a sympathetic ear. This was the catalyst that eventually led to the success story we have today. Since 2005 the EPCOR Britannia Mine Water Treatment Plant has been operating, paid in a large part by the mining companies who were classified as the previously responsible parties. The mine is used as a reservoir to store the polluted water before being passed through the treatment facility. The plant will need to operate in perpetuity. The site was once known as the worst single point discharge of metal pollution into a marine environment in North America. Today, life has returned to the intertidal zone and salmon and trout can be found in the lower reaches of Britannia Creek. What was once an embarrassment to the mining industry is now hailed as a shining example of how an abandoned mine can be reclaimed.

It is unlikely that the story ends here. In another ten years, more will of course have happened. Yet hopefully the ride will be a bit smoother, with things settling down for the community after its rebirth. What was once an isolated mining town is today an attractive community in the heart of a major tourism destination. The newer residents, many from Vancouver, have brought fresh perspectives, while those who have stayed throughout are proud of how they have helped shape the town's bright future.

Diane Mitchell

Curator of Education & Collections, Britannia Mine Museum

Jane Iverson

Britannia Beach resident and local historian

GEMS FROM TOWNSITE SOCIAL CLUB MINUTES
1929 - 1935

"Moved that the orchestra be paid five dollars apiece for three hours dance. Everything over the three hours the Club is not responsible for. Present – St. Laurent, Gaines, Jenkins, Myself, Evitts and Fitzpatrick."

"It was suggested Mrs. Touhey, Mrs. Jost, Mrs. Fulton, Mrs. Mitchell and Mrs. Dave MacDonald take charge of the supper."

"For Auditor, Mr. Davenport nominated by Lipsey, Mr. Gordon Thompson nominated by Ebbutt. Mr. Davenport withdrew his name. Being pressed for his objection by Mr. Lipsey, George said 'Because Mr. Thompson knew what he was doing half the time, whereas I don't'."

"The Ladies' Aid came under discussion owing to a misunderstanding with the Club Steward. It was decided to refund $1.00 to the Ladies' Aid for help which they paid for."

"Since the discontinuance of the movie, patronage of the library had increased by 33%."

"Sports – enthusiasm somewhat dampened by present smallpox restrictions." March 11th, 1932.

"Regarding the motion that a vaudeville turn might be put on at the Movie Hall, C. Johnson moved the proposal be postponed indefinitely, seconded by S.F. Bruce. Carried."

"Mr. D. Stewart suggested that as funds are needed to fix the pool tables, that players be charged. There was a lot of discussion on this subject. Mr. T. Mayes suggested that money be taken from the accident benefit fund for the pool room."

"There was much discussion concerning women on payroll paying Club dues. Deadlocked and layed over till the next meeting." February 18th, 1934.

"The new Constitution next came up for ratification. After a lot of discussion, it was found that the new constitution was missing. On motion by Mr. Mayes, seconded by Mr. Baggs, the meeting adjourned." April 16th, 1934.

"Kitchenette supper for Christmas discussed – to guarantee Mr. Bell $150.00, supper for 300 at 50 cents each." Nov. 26th, 1934.

"Moved by G. Mitchell, seconded by W. Baird, that $55.00 be appropriated for a dance on 24th May – admission 75 cents per couple." May 8th, 1935.

LEACHING OF COPPER BY PERCOLATING WATERS

The leaching process developed empirically as a commercial metal recovery medium some fifty or sixty years ago was originally thought to be effected through recognizable chemical reactions alone. In recent years, through biological research, the action of living bacteria has been found to contribute to the action which takes place. These bacteria are a variant of a common soil type, requiring oxygen and carbon dioxide for their growth process, but using iron, sulphur or the metallic sulphide compounds as their energy sources. In a suitable medium, which includes acid water with temperatures between 40 degrees and 98 degrees F., a good supply of air and the presence of copper sulphides, the bacteria will break down the complex ore bearing rock and free the metal for absorption into solution.

Precipitation is the process through which the metal is recovered from solution, which is passed over scrap iron in various forms, the best and most practical being scrap and salvage tin plate since it presents the largest surface in ratio to its weight, for exposure to the pregnant solution. In the exchange, metallic copper is released in solid granular form and the iron takes into solution – going to the tailings flume. Between two and three pounds of iron are required for each pound of copper recovered.

Up to 1963 some 27 million pounds of copper had been recovered from the Britannia workings by this method, chiefly from Fairview Mine above the 1050 level.

Ref. Chapter 6, Page 85.

STAFF

The word "staff" describes the whole working force, both salaried and hourly workers. Mr. C.P. Browning's efforts notwithstanding, in 1932 "The Staff was reduced from the high of 1100 men in 1928 to 548", see page 88. This refers to the entire crew.

NOTES FROM 1ST EDITION
BRITANNIA BEACH CENTENNIAL COMMITTEE

Chairman - J. C. S. Moore

Secretary-Treasurer - Mrs. A.T. (Mary) Smith

Members - Mr. W. B. Montgomery, Mrs. Allan (Betty) McNair, Mrs. Jack (Alice) Graney, Mrs. Fred (Olive) Baxter, Miss Joan Ehler, Mr. Dave Clark, Mr. Hugh Chisholm

---

Kathleen Malloy - Designer of this book cover, is a granddaughter of Dr. Menzies, medical officer at Beach 1917-24, including flood in 1921. See p. 60 and 61.

Photo credits - Frank Bruce and Provincial Archives.

Dan O'Connor - Master mechanic at Beach, Born in P.E.I. worked at Greenwood came to Britannia in 1913, made Master Mechanic in 1921.

Browning's Lake - Described in Chapter 9, page 128.

> The Lake! The jeweled lake that far from curious eyes,
> Embosomed by the hills, serene and secret lies.
> Here might have knelt Narcissus, while the breeze
> Mocked the faint voice of Echo in the trees.
>
> S. Frank Bruce, Britannia, 1932.

Images from 1967 - 1974, Anaconda

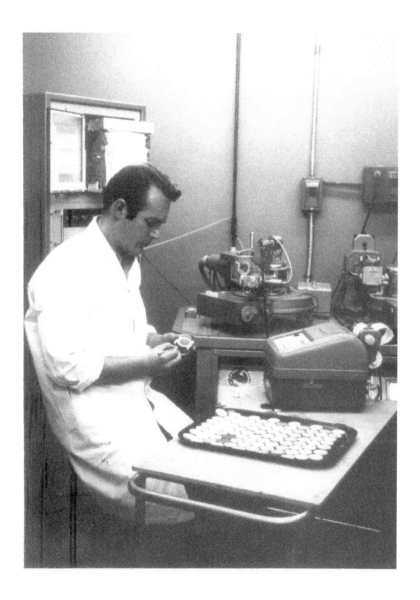

Asssayer. BMM #3604

May Day Celebrations. BMM #5157

Mine rescue and first aid competition. BMM #3594

Children in front of Mill 2. BMM #5554

Taking part in parade. BMM #6084

Using the stoper drill. BMM #5719

INDEX

Aboriginal contact 5, 6
Acid Rock Drainage - *See* Pollution
Anaconda Copper Company 105, 143
Beach Ladies Aid 132
Britannia Beach 1, 19, 20, 23, 25, 32-35, 37, 49-51, 53-55, 57, 78-80, 88-90, 92, 94, 102, 105, 112-114, 116-118
   Leatherdale tract 20
   Waterfront 126
Britannia Copper Syndicate 19-25, 32
Britannia Mine
   Bears 134, 137
   Camps - *See* Camps
   Community Clubs 127-130, 134
   Community spirit 112, 118, 143
   Company Town 127
   Copper Queen 128
   Dam, Utopia 35
   Dams 32, 55
   Dock 23
   Drought 49
   Early development 23
   Efficiency 80
   Exploration 20, 32, 53
   Firefighting 35
   Labor 32, 52, 53, 79, 81, 91
   Liquor 34, 126
   Mines - *See* Mines, Britannia
   Potential shut down 101, 103
   Production 50, 52, 53, 78, 79, 82, 91, 101, 103
   Recreation 33, 78, 125-127, 129-131, 135, 141-143
   Religion 135, 143
   Reopens, 1959 105
   Reputation 78
   Rivalry 129
   Shut down, 1958 103
   Telephone system 117, 138
   Theatre 139
   Zinc 82, 101
Britannia Mining & Smelting Company 18, 31, 67, 68, 75, 82, 104, 130
Britannia Mountain 35, 50
Britannia name, origin 3-8
Britannia Smelting Company 25, 31, 32
Buildings
   Barber Shop 50
   Bowling Alleys 78
   Brothel 33

Church 79, 135
Club House, Townsite 141
Company Store, Beach 23, 32, 33, 75, 76
Company Store, Cooperative 77
Company Store, Townsite 140, 141
Dance Hall 35
Engineering Office, Townsite 50
Foundry, Electric Furnace 79
Gymnasium 78, 79
Hospital, Beach 32
Hospital, Townsite 50, 140
Hotel, Beach 23, 33
Japanese bunkhouse 34, 53
Laundry Plant 35
Mill 1 22, 23, 51
Mill 2 32, 35, 49, 53
Mill 3 54, 78-80, 93
Powerhouse, Beach 23
Recreation Building, Townsite 50
Recreation Hall 51
Roller Rink 35
Sawmill, Victoria 53
School, Beach 79
School, Townsite 50, 140
Steam Plant 32
Swimming pools 130
Theatre, Beach 50, 131
Vanner 51
Camps
   Barbara 50, 131
   Daisy 113, 142
   Empress 112, 131, 134
   Halfway 116
   Jane (1050 Level) 19, 35, 36, 112
   Tunnel 35-37, 57
   Victoria 53, 78, 79, 112, 130, 131, 137
Canadian Institute of Mining and
   Metallurgy 80
Claims
   Empress 18
   Fairview 21
   First staked 17
   Goldsmith Copper Company 19
   Jane 17, 21
   Mineral Creek 21
   Queen 18
   Victoria 18
Copper precipitation
   Britannia Beach 78

Jane Flat Plant	77, 78
Method	77, 159
Mount Sheer Townsite	78
Copper Queen - *See* Britannia Mine (Copper Queen)	
Creeks	
Britannia	19, 23, 35, 55, 77
Furry	19, 53
Jane	19, 36
Mineral	19
Thistle	19
Disasters	
Cave in	54
Flood, 1921	55-58
Flood, 1991	153
Jane Slide	36-41, 49
Mill 2 fire	53
Firemen's Ball	132
Flu- *See* Influenza	
Frank Slide	36
Glory hole	22
Gold Rush	13, 81
Great Depression	79, 80
Howe Sound	4, 6, 13, 14, 17, 77, 112, 113, 126
Howe Sound Company	23-25, 32, 35, 81, 82, 100, 102-105
Calera Mining Company	25
Chelan Copper Mining Company	132
El Potosi Mining Company	25
Howmet Corporation	105
Salmon property, Idaho	102
Sherrit-Gordin nickel, Manitoba	103
Torbit Mining Company Ltd	79
Howe Sound Copper Mine	14
Influenza	51
International Geological Congress visit	34
Japanese community	
See Camps (Halfway)	
See Mount Sheer Townsite (Knobb Hill)	
See War (Japanese Internment)	
Workers	39, 114, 116
Knobb Hill	*See* Mount Sheer Townsite:Knobb Hill
Launders - *See* Copper precipitation	
Leaching - *See* Copper precipitation	
Lillooet Burrard Inlet Cattle Trail	15
Market	
Copper prices	34, 35, 52, 79-82, 102
Gold prices	81
Zinc prices	101, 102
Mines, Britannia	

Empress	35
Fairview	20, 35, 78
Jane	23
Mammoth Bluff	22, 23
Victoria	77
Mines, other	
Allenby	53
Anaconda	53
Anyox	53
Barkerville	81
Boundary District	53
Bralorne	81
Brooklyn	53
Cariboo Gold Quartz Mine	81
Copper Mountain	53
Deadwood	53
Gold Drop	53
Knobb Hill	53
Mother Lode	53
Old Ironside	53
Phoenix	53
Pioneer	81
Stemwinder	53
Mount Sheer Townsite	49, 50, 78, 79, 88, 102, 104, 105, 112, 114, 115, 117, 125, 134, 139-143
Knobb Hill	116
Snow	139
Newspapers	
Beachcomber, The	134
Britannia News	134
Britco News	130-134
Townsite Reporter	117, 134
Northwestern Smelting and Refining Company Ltd.	25
Ore deposit	20
Discovery	16, 17
Fairview mineral zone	20
Geology	1-2
Gold	53
Silver	53
Zinc	82
Payroll theft	102
People	
Adams, Christine	128
Adams, Joseph	19
Adams, L.	20
Adams, Mason T.	32
Adams, Norma	128
Adamson, Lila	128
Anderson, Marlene	128
Anderson, Mr. & Mrs. Aleck	56
Appleton, Mrs.	39

Bacon, Bert	56
Bacon, Mildren	128
Bagshawe, E.	132
Balderson, Jack	94
Barclay, Mary	57
Baxter, Henry	38
Beaton, Bill	132
Beer, Edeltraud	128
Bellinger, Herman C.	21, 25
Bing, Yip	51, 57
Bjorkman, L.	135
Black, John Keith	102
Black, Wesley	135
Bogle, Betty Lou	128
Bonthorne, Barclay	17, 18
Boscowitz & Sons	18, 19, 21, 25, 26
Boscowitz, Barbara	50
Boscowitz, David	18, 21
Boscowitz, Leopold	18, 21
Bower, George	20
Brace, R.	100
Bradley, Betty	128
Breen, J.	25
Browning, Carleton Perkins	50, 76-78, 80-82, 94, 101, 117, 127
Randolph Bruce Gold Medal	80
Browning, Emily	128
Browning, Mrs C.P.	93
Butters, Phil	136
Campanolla, Ernie	40
Campbell, George W.	23
Cates, Captain	19, 40, 112, 113
Ceppreley, H.T.	20
Chickasowa (known as)	115
Clark, Mabel	128
Clark, W.A.	17, 18
Copeland, C.E.	39
Curnow, Jim	54
Curnow, Tom	54
Cutler, Captain C.C.	68
Dalton, J.A.	100
Davis, Enid	128
Dawson, Bill	131
Deas, Jimmy	131
Dewdney, Edgar	21, 22, 24, 32, 50
Dick, Bob	138
Donohue, Edward Joseph	52, 53, 57, 75, 77
Donohue, Jackie	128
Dorner, Basil	54
Drysburgh, James	37
Dudley, Dr. W. F.	37
Dull, Charles M.	21, 32
Dunbar, Eleanor Jean	128
Dunn, Thomas	20
Dupuis, H.	36
Elliott, Linda	128
Emmott, Jim	55
Ferguson, Roy	100
Findlay, James	19
Fleming, Brenda	128
Fleming, Judy	128
Fleming, Sheila	128
Forbes, Dr. Alexander A.	15-17
Fraser, Lena	128
Freemand, C.	135
Furry, Oliver	17, 18, 21, 25, 26
Galbraith, T.	100
Goss, Barbara	128
Granger, dog fisherman	15, 16
Green, Eloise	128
Green, Mrs	132
Greenlee, Barney B.	105
Haig, Fred	137
Hamilton, Bert	133
Hewson, Mrs. A.	132
Hill, Nancy	128
Hills, J.T.	19
Hornton, Fred	137
Humphreys, John F.	20
Hurley, Pat	128
Ivey, Bill	131
Jackson, Elizabeth	128
Johnson, 'Hardrock'	138
Keith, J.C.	18
Kendall, J.D.	21
King, Bert	55
Kirkland, A.G.	105
Knight, M.	135
Labelle, J.	100
Langerquist, P.A.	130
Leach, R.H.	32
Lee, J.W.	20, 21
Leonard, F.M.	20
Lindley, Karen	128
Lonon, William	55
Lord Bessborough	81
Lord Willingdon	78, 81
Louther, Mrs. W.	132
Lowther, Amstrong 'Slim'	133
Lowther, Winifred	133
MacDonald, John Keith - *See* People (Black, John Keith)	
Madore, Agnes	128
Malm, John	113
Marshall, D.G.	32

Martin, Joseph	26	Russell, Pearl	128
Matheson, Eleanor-Ann	128	Ryan, Bob	51
Matheson, W.A.	77	Sanders, Jacqueline	128
Mathiesen, Mr. & Mrs. Archie	57	Sarles, N.	100
Mathiesen, Vera	57	Schley, E.B.	50, 76, 80, 82, 102
McClelland, G.C.	100	Schley, Grant Barney	22, 31, 32, 50, 52
McCullough, Thomas	39		
McDonald, Donald	37	Schley, Reeve Jr.	102, 104
McGaw, Winnie	132	Scott, Geordie	132
McGregor, Donald	104	Scott, Joan	128
McIntosh, Andy	132	Settle, Faye	128
McKenzie, Jack	88	Sherriff, Brownie	135
McKenzie, Kathleen	128	Sherriff, Charles	137
McKenzie, N.	100	Skookum (known as)	116
McKenzie, Roy	88	Smith, Ken	94
McKenzie, Thelma	128	Snider, Paul	132
McLarnin, Jimmy	133	Spaden, Alex	94
McLeod, Carol	128	Spence, M.T.	37
McMeekin, Charles W.	19, 21, 26	Stern, Henry	22-24
McNeill, C.B.	32	Stewart, L.G.	135
Menzies, Dr. A.M.	56, 57	Sullivan, Patsy	128
Mitchell, George	139	Thionen, M.	57
Moodie, John Wedderburn Dunbar 32-35, 51, 52, 75, 116, 126		Thompson, Jack	133
		Trythall, Betty	135
Moore, J.I.	137	Turner, Thomas	25
Moore, Mr. & Mrs.	132	Valentine, C.J.	21
Morse, C.F.	40	Vancouver, Captain George	4-7, 13
Munroe, A.C.	79	Vollans, Elizabeth	128
Munroe, Buddy	132	Walbran, Captain John	66
Munroe, Sybil	132	Walters, Howard S.	19-21
Murphy, Harvey	94	Weaver, William M. Jr.	104
Murphy, Miss	56	Welby, Margaret	128
Newberry, Edith	128	Wharton, Doris	128
Newell, Marlene	128	White, Y.M.	32
Nicholson, Olga	128	Wylie, W.A.	40
Nieding, B.B.	52, 76	Yates, Captain	113
Owen, Mrs A.W.	39	Places	
Park, Stanley	40	Anvil Island	5, 6
Perkins, Sam	137	Boundary Bay	3
Perry, C.	40	Britannia Beach - *See* Britannia Beach main entry	
Peterson, Elaine	56		
Peterson, Mr. & Mrs. George	56	Britannia Mountain	16, 18
Phillips, Verna	128	Browning Lake	117, 126, 142
Poulton,W.	100	Crofton	25
Pringle, D.W.	105	Fairy Falls	20
Quigly, W.J.	77	Hopkins Landing	16
Rand, C.D.	20	Howe Sound - *See* Howe Sound main entry	
Richardson, Skip	132		
Roach, Georgina	128	McNab Creek	17
Robinson, George H.	21, 22, 25, 31	Minaty Bay	116, 117
Roper, Edward Cecil	100, 101, 104, 118	Mount Elphinstone	16
		Mount Sheer - *See* Mount Sheer Townsite main entry	
Roper, Winnifred	128		

168

Mountain Lake 142
Pettgill Lake 142
Phantom Lake 117, 126
Roberts City 13
Squamish - *See* Mount Sheer Townsite main entry
Texada Island 17
Townsite - *See* Mount Sheer Townsite main entry
Vancouver, trips to 142
Woodfibre - *See* Woodfibre main entry
Pollution 126, 153, 157
Railways
   Canadian Pacific Railway 15, 68, 113
   Pacific Great Eastern Railway 18, 35, 112, 118
Safety 89-90
   National Safety Council 95
   St. John Ambulance 90
Shipping
   Ballena 37, 40, 126
   Bowena 113
   Britannia 113
   Burt 19
   Canadian Pacific Navigation Company 68, 113
   Capilano 113
   Cheam 113
   Defiance 19, 112, 113
   Early years 19
   Lady Alexandra 113
   Lady Cecilia 113
   Lady Cynthia 113
   Lady Evelyn 113
   Lady Rose 113
   North Pacific 67
   Olympic 67, 68
   Princess Louise 66-68
   Quadra 66-68, 71
   Quadra Steamship Company 68
   Saturna 18
   Terminal Steam Navigation Company 19, 40, 112
   Union Steamship Company 112, 113
Skip, The - *See* Transportation (Incline Railway)
Smelters

Boundary Falls 53
Crofton 25
Grand Forks 53
Greenwood 53
Tacoma 66, 68
Squamish 35, 113, 114, 117, 118, 126, 129, 130, 135, 142
Transportation
   Aerial tramway, Riblet 22, 34, 51, 114, 115
   Beach to Townsite road 117, 118, 143
   Daisy Trail 19, 33
   Dock 23
   East Howe Sound Stage Company 118
   Horses 114
   Incline Railway 114, 118, 141
   Mine railway 23, 116
   Narrow gauge railway 115, 141
   Pier, early 19
   Squamish to Britannia 117
   Tramways 23, 32
   Vancouver highway 112, 118
   Wharf 35
Tunnel Townsite - *See* Mount Sheer Townsite
Union 33, 88-90, 94
   Industrial Workers of the World/ Wobblies 33, 88
   Local 663 95
   Strike 105
   Strike, B.C. 101
   Strike, Japanese workers 89
   Women's Auxiliary 95
War
   A.R.P. (Air Raid Precautions) 92, 93
   Air raid shelter 93
   Imperial Munitions Board 50
   Japanese Internment 91, 92
   Korean War 101
   Pacific Coast Militia Rangers 92
   Pearl Harbor 91, 92
   Red Cross Corps 93, 127, 143
   World War I 49, 51
   World War II 82, 90, 91, 100
Whalen Pulp and Paper Company 68
Woodfibre 68, 114, 129, 135, 142

CPSIA information can be obtained
at www.ICGtesting.com
Printed in the USA
LVHW041937110719
623836LV00001B/1/P